When I'm Out of Staying Human
Hanna Komar

Hanna Komar,
When I'm Out of Here: Staying Human in a Dictator's Jail

design: odren alina
translation: Hanna Komar and John Farndon
copyediting: Alana Felton
photo: Violetta Savchits

ISBN 978-1-915601-83-4

Copyright © Hanna Komar, 2025
Copyright © odren alina, book design, 2025

SKARYNA PRESS

Acknowledgements

First of all, I would like to thank everyone who shared their experience for this book. It was an immense act of trust, and I hope I didn't fail you.

Secondly, I'm very grateful for the support I received while writing the original version of the book. I finished the first draft during my four-week stay at the Baltic Centre for Writers and Translators in Visby, Sweden. I had the space and resources to revise it and prepare it for publication during another four-week residency — this time at the Next Page Foundation's Literature and Translation House in Sofia, Bulgaria.

The original book was published with the financial support of the European Union as part of the EU4Culture project. This funding allowed us to donate all proceeds from sales to initiatives supporting Belarusians facing persecution.

I'm deeply grateful to Skaryna Press for supporting both the original and the translation, and for believing in this project unconditionally.

This book wouldn't have been possible without the creative energy of my friend and designer odren alina.

The copyediting help provided by Alana Felton was invaluable.

And finally, to John Farndon for his faith in my writing and translation — and for not allowing me to give up.

To everyone who heard about the original book and encouraged me to publish the translation — I hope it won't disappoint you.

About the author

Hanna Komar is a Belarusian poet, writer, translator and performer based in London. An activist who participated in the post-election protests of 2020, she has been living in exile since 2021.

Hanna is a member of PEN Belarus and an honorary member of English PEN. She is a joint recipient of the 2020 Freedom of Speech Prize from the Norwegian Authors' Union. She is now working on a PhD, exploring how poetry can give voice to women's experiences of domestic abuse and state violence. Her work uncovers the connections between the two and opens space for resistance.

About the translators

Hanna Komar

Hanna's experience as a translator spans literary, documentary, and advocacy work, with projects ranging from poetry and essays to subtitles for human rights documentaries. She has co-translated Charles Bukowski's poems into Belarusian, translates her own poetry into English, and contributes to international projects such as Free All Words, bringing contemporary Belarusian and Ukrainian voices to global audiences. Translating her own words — and the voices of others who shared this journey — became a process of healing, reflection, and renewed commitment to making these stories accessible to a wider audience. Hanna hopes this translation offers readers not only insight into Belarus's struggle, but also a sense of the resilience and community that sustained those who lived it.

John Farndon

John Farndon is a best-selling author of maybe 2000 non-fiction books, and also a playwright, songwriter, poet and an award-winning translator of literary works from many different languages, including Arabic, Kazakh, Uzbek and Tajik. He has been particularly active in translating work from poets in Belarus and Ukraine, in conjunction, for instance, with the Free All Words project. Since February 2022, he has translated hundreds of Ukrainian poems and over 40 new Ukrainian plays for the Worldwide Ukrainian Playreading Project, including Neda Nejdana's Pussycat in Memory of Darkness (Offies Finalist Best New Play), and Inna Goncharova's The Trumpeter, staged at London's Finborough and on tour. He is the joint winner of the 2024 Ukrainian Literature in Translation prize for his translation of Falling by the late Maksym Kryvtsov; joint winner of the 2019 European Bank RD Literature prize for Hamid Ismailov's Devil's Dance; 2020 Finalist US Pen Translation award for Rollan Sesyenbaev's The Dead Wander in the Desert.

Table of Contents

Note on Transliteration	10
Glossary	12
Foreword	19
Tuesday, 8 September	37
Wednesday, 9 September	112
Thursday, 10 September	145
Friday, 11 September	164
Saturday, 12 September	179
Sunday, 13 September	192
Monday, 14 September	203
Tuesday, 15 September	216
Wednesday, 16 September	228
Thursday, 17 September	238

The section of the wall at Mašerava Avenue in Minsk where the author was arrested.

in our prison cell
the four of us
share everything:
liquid white
and sticky ochre light
bed squeaking
the cold curling up
the sun behind the thick window
fresh air from the gaps
between window frames
free trains rumbling
iron doors clashing
tapping against the wall
'long-live-be-la-rus'
warm water in the shower
deodorant
a newspaper with crossword puzzles
the voice reading aloud
thickened time
questions
curses
nightmares
and the very words
'when i'm out of here...'

Note on Transliteration

The traditional Belarusian Latin alphabet — łacinka — is best suited for transliterating Belarusian words and names. It was once the standard for transliterating Belarusian geographical names and anthroponyms, yet was suppressed by Russian authorities in the nineteenth century. Since then, alternative transliteration (romanisation) systems have been adopted, with or without input from Belarusians. Among these, the most commonly used is the BGN/PCGN system, developed by Americans and the British.

In independent Belarus, an effort was made to develop a transliteration system for geographical names based on łacinka (e.g., Homieĺ instead of the Russian Gomel; Hrodna instead of the Polish Grodno). This system, known as the Instruction on Transliteration of Belarusian Geographical Names with Latin Script Letters, was recommended by the United Nations Group of Experts on Geographical Names (UNGEGN).

After 2020, however, Belarusian authorities largely abandoned łacinka and adopted Russian-style romanisation systems, even for personal names. Additionally, some Belarusians use Russian-language versions of their names for Latin-script transliterations (e.g., Olga instead of Volha). Despite the publisher's efforts to maintain consistency, a plurality of transliterations from Cyrillic alphabets could not be avoided in this publication. For well-known individuals — Maryia Kalesnikava, Sviatlana Tsikhanouskaya — we used the spellings preferred by the individuals themselves or by human rights organisations. Russian words are spelled according to commonly used conventions. In all other cases, the Belarusian łacinka system was used.

In this book, we use łacinka not only for geographical names but for most Belarusian words and names. Belarusian łacinka is easy to grasp, and here are a few notes on some letters:

- **C** as ts in cats.
- **H** as h in Henry.
- **J** as y in Roy.
- **Y** as i in Chris.
- **I** as i in Bill.

Some consonants have diacritics, which slightly alter their pronunciation:

- **č** as **ch** in church.
- **š** as **sh** in shoes.
- **ž** as **s** in pleasure.
- **ć, ś, ń, ź** are soft versions of **c, n, s,** and **z.**

Combinations of **i** or **j** with **a, e, o,** or **u** create new sounds, like **ya** (yah), **ye** (yet), **yo** (yonder), and **yu** (tune).

Glossary

Administrative arrest
In Belarus, administrative arrest is a form of state detention that over 50,000 Belarusians have experienced for participating in peaceful protests since 2020. Penalties include fines and imprisonment ranging from several days to months of repeated incarceration without a fair trial.

Akrescina
(Russian spelling: Okrestina). A detention centre in Minsk where tens of thousands of Belarusians have been jailed for participating in protest activities following the 2020 presidential campaign. Detainees kept there experience ill-treatment, torture and inhumane conditions.

Base amount
A national reference amount used in Belarus to maintain the consistency of pensions, scholarships, social welfare payments, duties, taxes, and fines in legal texts, regardless of inflation. In 2020, fines were calculated based on this measure, with one base amount set at 27 BYN (approximately 9 GBP).

Being water
A metaphor from the protest — the tactic of "being water" meant being prepared to change the route of the protest marches spontaneously across several locations. It originated in Hong Kong in 2019 and 2020 when protesters used the slogan "Be Water" to describe their ability to stay flexible and quickly adapt to evade arrest yet coordinate activities in various places.

The Berkut
The Berkut was a special police (riot police) unit in Ukraine. Initially specialised in fighting organised crime, it transitioned to operating semi-autonomously and was used in repressive activities against Ukrainian citizens who opposed Yanukovych in the 2004 presidential election. The Berkut committed violence against protesters during the Maidan Uprising of 2013–2014 and was held responsible for most of the deaths known as the Heavenly Hundred when 107 Ukrainian civilians were killed during the protests, in February 2014. The Berkut was dissolved as an agency in Ukraine on 25 February 2014.

DJs of Change
Uladź Sakaloŭski and Kiryl Halanaŭ, sound engineers from the Minsk State Children and Youth Palace, were assigned to work at a pro-government event during the presidential election campaign on 6 August 2020 in Minsk. Instead of playing pro-regime music, they put on "Peremen" ("Changes") by the late Soviet-era rock musician Viktor Tsoi. The song has become a symbol for Belarusians longing for political and social change. The DJs' act was heartily welcomed by Belarusians, and Uladź and Kiryl became a symbol of the protest movement, dubbed "the DJs of Change."

Fryzura
Belarusian for "hairstyle." The person spoke in Russian all the time, except for this word.

Glass
A metal box inside a police van, designed for one person.

Gopnik
A term used to describe a young man (or woman — gopnitsa) of urban working-class background in Russia, Ukraine, Belarus and other former Soviet republics. The stereotypical image of a gopnik is someone who is conservative, aggressive, homophobic, nationalist and racist, and who holds strong anti-Western views.

GUBOPiK
The Main Directorate for Combating Organised Crime and Corruption of the Ministry of Internal Affairs of the Republic of Belarus (GUBOPiK) is a state security service involved in numerous acts of political repression, violence and torture against political opponents of Lukashenka's regime.

"He also says he trusts the teachers at the school…"
During presidential elections in Belarus, polling stations are often located in schools, and teachers are recruited as members of electoral commissions. In the 2020 election, many teachers were believed to have participated in election fraud.

Henadzieŭna
Patronymic name derived from Henadziy.

"I automatically take shoelaces…"
In prison, shoelaces are removed to prevent prisoners using them as a weapon to harm oneself or others.

Kamaroŭka
A market in central Minsk. Leading up to the 2020 presidential election, it became a venue for collecting signatures for alternative candidates and holding electoral pickets. After the election, it became a popular site for political demonstrations. The first women's protests were held there.

Karpiankoŭ
Mikałaj Karpiankoŭ (Russian spelling: Nikolay Karpenkov), Deputy Minister of Internal Affairs and incumbent Commander of Internal Troops of Belarus since November 2020, is responsible for inhumane and degrading treatment of peaceful protesters, including arbitrary arrest and detention.

Kupalinka
A popular Belarusian song described as the "musical business card of Belarus." Its lyrical heroine, the Kupała Night Maiden, is "weeding a rose, piercing her white hands," "plucking flowers, weaving wreaths, and shedding tears." Both the poet Michaś Čarot, who wrote the lyrics, and composer Uladzimier Teraŭski were executed during Stalin's purges of the late 1930s. Kupalinka became one of the main protest songs in 2020.

Maryia Kalesnikava
(Russian spelling: Maria Kolesnikova). A Belarusian professional flutist and political activist. During the 2020 presidential elections, she led Viktar Babaryka's campaign and later became part of Sviatlana Tsikhanouskaya's united campaign. On 7 September, she was kidnapped by unidentified law enforcement officers. She tore up her passport when pressured to leave Belarus. On 6 September 2021, she was sentenced to 11 years in a penal colony for her political activity and released on 13 December 2025.

Maršrutka
A type of public transportation in Eastern Europe and the former Soviet Union — a cross between a bus and a taxi, often operating as minibuses on set routes.

Moon
Prison slang for the dim night light kept on in cells for surveillance purposes.

"Mury"
The song "Mury" (Belarusian for "walls") holds a powerful symbolic meaning for the Belarusian protest movement of 2020–2021. Originally written by Polish singer-songwriter Jacek Kaczmarski in 1978, "Mury" became an anthem for Solidarity, the Polish opposition movement. It was based on a Catalan song by Lluís Llach called "L'Estaca", which also symbolised resistance against dictatorship. "Mury" was translated into Belarusian by the Belarusian poet Andrei Khadanovich. It was adopted by protestors because its lyrics resonate deeply with the struggle for freedom, justice, and collective solidarity. The refrain goes like this: "Tear down these prison walls! / You want your freedom, take it all! / The wall will soon crumble, crumble, crumble, / And we'll see the old world fall! (Tr. By Simon Lewis, "'Tear Down These Prison Walls!' Verses of Defiance in the Belarusian Revolution").

"Nature has cleansed itself so much that 2010 is returning to Belarus."
A record-breaking number of 10 presidential candidates were registered for the 2010 election in Belarus.

OMON
(Belarusian: AMAP). The OMON are the riot police frequently sent to violently suppress the protests. They wear all-black (or unmarked green) uniform and balaclavas. To conceal their identities and to avoid reprisals.

OSVOD
The Belarusian Republican Society for Water Rescue. During the dispersion of a peaceful Sunday march on 7 September 2020 in Minsk, several protesters jumped into Kamsamolskaje Lake to escape from the police. OSVOD rescuers picked them up and transported them to the opposite shore. They were later detained and put on trial for it.

"Perhaps you yourself are the red lights of the lighthouse…"
A line from the poem "Perhaps You Yourself are the Red Light of the Lighthouse" by Kateřina Rudčenková, published in Modern Poetry in Translation, No. 2 (2020).

Rasolnik
(Russian spelling: rassolnik). A traditional soup commonly found in Belarusian cuisine made with pickled cucumbers and pearl barley, either with meat or vegetarian.

Razmaŭlajem
Belarusian for "speaking." The person spoke in Russian all the time, except for this word.

Salo
(Belarusian: sała). Salted or cured slabs of pork fat, traditional in Belarus. It's similar to bacon in appearance but doesn't have much (or any) meat on it, and it's not fried before eating.

Sanatoryj
A state-run health resort offering treatments such as mineral baths, mud therapy and physiotherapy. These Soviet-era institutions follow strict daily routines, including scheduled meals and treatments. Many still have Soviet-style interiors, basic amenities and a focus on affordability rather than luxury.

Siłaviki
(Pl. Russian spelling: siloviki). Members of the Belarusian military, police or intelligence services.

Star balm
Golden Star Balm (Zviozdochka), known from Soviet times for its strong menthol smell and warming effect. Used to treat headaches, runny nose, flu, dizziness and motion sickness. In prison it helped to mask the smell of the cell toilet.

Suški
Small, crunchy, mildly sweet bread rings that originated in Eastern Europe, often eaten with tea or coffee for dessert.

Terrorists
The regime labels many activists — both political prisoners and those in exile — as "terrorists," misusing anti-terrorism and anti-extremism laws to silence ordinary political activity and expression.

The Pahonia
The Pahonia was the coat of arms of the Grand Duchy of Lithuania, a medieval state that included the lands of modern-day Belarus. It translates to "the chase" and depicts "a knight on a rearing horse". After Belarus declared independence from the Soviet Union in 1991, its Parliament adopted the Pahonia as the official coat of arms. In June 1995, authoritarian president Aliaksandr Lukashenka replaced it with a modified Soviet emblem following a falsified and illegal referendum. Since then, the Pahonia has been one of the symbols of Belarusians' democratic aspirations and resistance to the regime. It was widely used by the protesters in 2020; displaying it in Belarus is now illegal.

Valadarka
(Russian spelling: Volodarka) Former Detention Centre No. 1 (SIZO No. 1) in Minsk, also known as Piščalaŭski Castle. The popular name Vaładarka was coined after the October Revolution when the street on which the building stood was renamed in honour of the revolutionary leader Vaładarski. It is a feared symbol of repression in Belarusian cultural memory and had been used as a pre-trial detention centre for arrested political activists.

Vieršy
Belarusian for "poems." The rest of the message was written in Russian.

Viasna
Human Rights Centre Viasna documented political repression and compiled lists of detainees during the 2020 protests.

Vkontakte
A Russian social media platform similar to Facebook that is popular in Russian-speaking countries, also in Belarus.

"Walks"
"I'm simply walking!" was a reply that Nina Bahinskaja, a prominent pro-democracy activist in Belarus, used when police officers tried to stop her in Minsk as she walked with a white-red-white flag during the 2020 protests. Her defiant reply became iconic and inspired many. Since then, we've referred to our marches as "walks."

"Why do you say narmalna"
The officer, speaking Russian, picked on my use of Belarusian. Narmalna is the Belarusian word for "fine" or "OK." Its pronunciation matches the Russian word with the same meaning. He questioned whether I was speaking Belarusian correctly.

Zmahary
Belarusian for "fighters." In Lukashenka's propaganda slang, zmahary refers to pro-democracy Belarusians. A Belarusian analogue of "Banderites" from anti-Ukrainian propaganda.

Žodzina
(Russian spelling: Zhodino). A prison in the town of Žodzina in the Minsk voblasc, where many protesters were detained and subjected to inhumane conditions and torture after the 2020 election.

Žy-vie-bie-ła-ruś
Zhyve Belarus! (literally, "Long live Belarus!") is a historic Belarusian patriotic slogan, widely used in 2020. It was coined by the Belarusian classic poet Janka Kupała in one of his poems from 1905–1907.

")" and "))"
In Belarusian digital communication, the closing parenthesis — ")" or repeated as "))" — is commonly used as a form of emoji to express warmth, friendliness, or a smile. Unlike the Western use of emoticons such as ":)", the Belarusian convention omits the eyes, relying solely on the curved brackets. The more brackets used, the stronger the emotional tone — for example, ")))" conveys more enthusiasm or affection than a single ")"

Foreword

I knew you would   want to write this…

And so I wrote…

To understand — my own experience, and myself as part of the collective one.

In Belarus, the same dictator, Aliaksandr Lukashenka, has been in power for over 30 years, since 1994. The fraudulent presidential election on 9 August 2020 was followed by the largest mass peaceful protests in Belarusian history, met with unprecedented police brutality and systemic repression. At the time of this publication, over 1,200 political prisoners remain behind bars. Over 8,000 individuals have faced politically motivated criminal prosecution, and over 50,000 have experienced arbitrary detentions. All of them have been subjected to ill-treatment; psychological, physical and sexual violence; torture and other inhumane conditions. I was one of the 50,000. This is my story.

I was detained on 8 September 2020. It was when we were marching in support of Maryia Kalesnikava and other activists detained around that time. The extraordinary Maryia Kalesnikava was a professional flautist who became the head of Viktar Babaryka's presidential campaign, and was one of the key figures of the fight against Lukashenka. Our march happened right the day after Maryia was suddenly kidnapped in the centre of Minsk by unidentified law enforcement officers. During the night, they took her to the Belarusian-Ukrainian border to deport her forcibly. But at the border crossing, Maryia tore up her passport, got out through the car window and walked towards the Belarusian border. They took her to prison and after a "trial" a year later condemned her to 11 years. Maryja was released on 13 December 2025.

Later in the day of the border incident, protesters gathered at various locations in Minsk in support of her. The march I attended was the largest. We were surrounded by the security forces which came out in large numbers, armed and masked, to break up the protest. By the evening, more than a hundred marchers had been grabbed forcibly and thrust into police vans to be taken off to prison — many of them women, including me. The targeting of women like that was new and seemed a turning point for us. After that, mass detentions of women were common at every women's protest.

After a cold anxious night at a Pieršamajski police department, I was brought before a court the following day, still hoping for some justice. With little evidence but the police statement, the so-called court sentenced me to nine days of administrative arrest. I spent two days in Akrescina prison and then was transferred to the prison in Žodzina, where I received a care package from my friends outside. In that package, my flatmate and ally Alena included a little notebook, so, I kept a diary of my time in prison. It was difficult, but I forced myself to write down something — anything — even just dry observations and facts. Activities. Details. Thoughts. This was my way of finding meaning in what was happening. "You are a poet, a writer," I thought to myself, "you are here anyway, and this is a unique experience: you can see this place, the one you've heard so much about, from the inside. You must write about it."

At first, I imagined this would be a slim book about my own experience, but for six months after my release, I couldn't even open that notebook. Then, on the day the court sentenced the journalists Katsiaryna Andrejeva and Darya Chultsova to two years in prison, I realised that as long as I was free, I had no right to remain silent. I had to tell this story. But telling only my own story felt wrong. I was also at a loss for words — my psyche refused to let me go deeper. At that time, I read The Unwomanly Face of War by Svetlana Alexievich. And so I began to collect voices, as she did.

Those nine days I spent in prison no longer seem like such a terrible experience, especially compared to the violence of early August 2020 and the later waves of repressions and torture. But this book should remain a testimony to what we lived through — both injustice and solidarity.

This book is also my way of expressing gratitude to the people with whom I shared this experience — not only during those days, but during the long months of resistance that followed. To the people who showed me what dignity, courage and solidarity truly mean — not in the romanticised or heroic sense I once imagined.

I finished the first draft in June 2021, but it was still raw. Some things remained unspoken, and something wasn't working. I realised that the problem was me — I wasn't being totally honest. I was avoiding my own character, almost silencing her voice.

It took me almost another six months to understand why I couldn't open up. The truth is, when I was released after nine days in prison, I felt that people around me saw me as a kind of hero. I received enormous support, which I believed was disproportionate to my small act of civil resistance.

A huge number of people had gone — and are still going — through much more difficult ordeals. I compared myself to them and couldn't allow myself to acknowledge that what I'd experienced was traumatising. I believed I had no right to show weakness, to show that I wasn't the strongest or the most generous, that I wasn't the embodiment of resourcefulness, wisdom or dignity that I admire so much in others.

In September 2021, I went to do an MA in London and wrote a play exploring my prison experience. While researching for the play, I came across the prison diary of British suffragette Katie Gliddon, who was imprisoned in Holloway in 1912. She described a young girl in a nearby cell who was beating around her cell like a bird. Katie, who knew what she was getting into, felt a lot of compassion for that girl. Two years after my release, we held a reading of the play in London. I heard Katie's quote read aloud, and I suddenly recognised myself in that scared little creature. And for the first time I allowed myself to be that. I felt relieved.

One can devalue their experience retrospectively. But what I did on the evening when I was detained, was the right thing. It was a test of my values, a test of maturity: somewhere inside I made a decision, and in the face of an existential choice, I made one — an irrational one — but one I am not ashamed of.

Some of the girls I interviewed for the book also recalled that moment of choice. One rushed after her boyfriend and later couldn't understand why, realising she might have been more useful had she stayed free. Another ran from the opposite side of the street to help us. She didn't even reach us — she was thrown into a police van. Once she had calmed down, she couldn't comprehend what had happened — she had always considered herself a rational person.

This book is an attempt to preserve that turning point in our history and share it with those who might find something moving or inspiring in it. It's an attempt to understand and accept my vulnerability.
A tribute to everyone who was there.

To everyone who was there.

Hanna Komar, London, 2025

Mid-May 2020. Several presidential candidates appear out of the blue. The internet is awash with jokes:

"Nature has cleansed itself so much that 2010 is returning to Belarus."

"Trump has announced that he doesn't know yet whether he'll participate in the elections in Belarus. Too many competitors."

"Belarus is still at peak registration for presidential candidates. At the end of July, a plateau should be reached and, after 9 August, a sharp decrease in the number of active candidates at large."

"Who are all these people?" I'm writing a message to a friend. "I don't know who to trust."

"Well, we know exactly who not to trust," she replies.

I was released from Žodzina prison a day ago.
To those who asked what to take to the prisoners, here we go)

What you should take to prisoners
or
'must haves' for 15 days of arrest

The authors are girls who were imprisoned in Akrescina and Žodzina, detained on 1.09.2020 for political reasons:

██████████████ and ██████ ██████████

Thank you for your help with the compilation:
██████████████████,
███████████████████,
████████████████

On 31 May I wrote on my Instagram, "If you considered leaving here at least once, all this concerns you."

Kamaroŭka. A kilometre-long queue of people who want to add their signature endorsing alternative candidates for the presidency. The air is saturated with hope and uplift I've never experienced before. My friends and I in activist circles aren't the only ones who want change.

1. Clothes, etc.

underwear — 2 pairs, min.

socks HIGH (2 pairs, cotton, 1 pair warm)

a t-shirt that you can tuck into trousers (thin, to dry not too long after wash, you sweat from stress and the mattresses in Akrescina have a very unpleasant smell, and it feels disgusting to touch them with your skin), — 1 long-sleeve, 1 short-sleeve

comfy trousers (keep it in mind that the laces will be cut)

warm sweatshirt or a HOODIE (a hoodie is preferable as the pillows in Akrescina stink, and there may be lice), that's comfortable and not too hot to sleep in

slippers (for the shower and elsewhere, as the inmates' shoelaces are removed from their shoes and it's really uncomfortable to walk the stairs and to the toilet)

a wireless bra for women (bras with underwire are taken away at the inspection and you have to keep your hands behind your back in the presence of males)

18 June — I'm at home: working, doing small things. In the evening, I open the news and see that people have formed a long living chain from the TsUM all the way down to the Circus. Something inside doesn't allow me to think for too long, I get dressed, put a few extra things into my backpack and run to Independence Avenue.
My first ever solidarity chain.

2. Hygiene items, etc.

toothbrush
toothpaste
universal soap (preferably liquid with a dispenser (if allowed), suitable both for the body and washing up)
deodorant / antiperspirant
moisturizer (after you wash the floor or toilet with chlorine, your hands are very dry)

plastic/wooden comb
hair elastic
toilet paper
antibacterial wet wipes

towel

sanitary pads/tampons
shampoo
nail file (cardboard base with round edges)
hair conditioner
cotton pads + micellar water
face wash
cotton buds

The next day, I come to the Pieršamajski District Court to support people I don't know, who've been charged with committing politically motivated crimes. This is how I become an independent observer in the courts for a few months. We help document violations and collect information about convictions.

3. Other useful things

a letter with kind words (you can write in a book to reduce the likelihood of confiscation)
cheap wristwatch (we never knew what time it was)

stamped envelopes (red express mail envelopes are best)
sheets of paper / notepad / notebook
2 pens/pencil
a couple of plastic-paper cups (because hot tea is poured into aluminium mugs without a handle, it's too hot to hold in your hands)

anything that can be used as an air freshener (such as car air fresheners, etc.)
Zvezdochka balm / something else so you don't smell the toilet
sleep mask (often the night light is very bright)
earplugs (you can't sleep because of the guard dogs barking)

blanket (in Akrescina, blankets have a very unpleasant smell)
paperback books (books of a political nature are confiscated, so choose your literature wisely. For example, I wasn't allowed 1984 by George Orwell)
card games (UNO, cards, Mafia, charades, etc)

sponge for washing dishes
brush to clean the sink/toilet
washing liquid
several extra bags (garbage/bag)

cigarettes for smokers

From 4 to 8 August, I sit in the corridor under the room for early voting at the polling station at 31A V. Charužaj Street and try to count how many people voted early. A guy from another polling station, who came by for some document, said, "Women will change the country forever this summer."

4. FOOD

cut everything into large pieces and put in packaging in plastic bags

nuts
dried fruits (seedless)

crackers
chips
crispbread
sliced brown / white bread (only in the very first package — maximum half a loaf, after that, no need)
sausage
salo

biscuits
wafers
chocolate
candies (chewing, chocolate, etc.)
jellies
chocolate bars (Snickers, etc.)

sometimes apples and pears are allowed

If you stand with your back to the Museum of the Great Patriotic War on the night of 9 August 2020, you can see me walking down from the bridge at the Niamiha river, where I'd just seen dozens of men in uniform, protected by body armour and shields, attacking several hundred peaceful protesters with water cannons and beating them with batons before arresting them. Some of my friends are running away from stun grenades and tear gas in a different part of Minsk.

Several buildings away from mine there is a row of the OMON, still and cold like the orders they execute.

WATER

— in sealed bottles (only for Akrescina, in Žodzina the water is good)

11 August, the day is as beautiful as our hopes for the better, but we already know about the thousands detained on the two previous nights, fifty people in a cell for four, one bottle of water for all, no food. Women listening to men being beaten, tortured and raped with batons next door. It's 5:30 pm; Siarhei and I are coming back to our apartment by bus. "Get off at the next stop," he says to me because, in my bag, I have the leaflets encouraging workers to go on strike, and we know that if the OMON find them, I may become the fifty-first person in a cell for four after being raped right in the police van. He gets off at the Stella, by the OMON checkpoint, and we can't find him for the next two days until he calls from the hospital. Head injury, multiple bruises, black eye, broken cheekbone, lung's hit... I can cry for the first time since 9 August.

ATTENTION!
Include several pairs of the most necessary things so that your loved ones can share them with those who didn't receive their packages yet, for example:

underwear
high socks
toothbrush
toilet paper
soap

On 12 August I wake up very sick, I got sick suddenly, literally overnight. "That must be the end of my revolution..." I think to myself. Already on 10 August, I realised I'm not a warrior: I can neither fight nor even run fast. What can I do?

News channels report that near Kamaroŭka, women in white clothes demand an end to the violence. I wasn't even wearing white clothes on that cold, autumn-like day. No flowers, no flags. I rush to the women, to get there in time. I have questions about the white clothes and the image of femininity. I'm not even certain I support peaceful protest. I don't need flowers, and with them, I want to say only one thing,

"I'm with you, sisters."

Here I stand, among these women, turning my head right and left, trying to comprehend where I am, trying to see those around me, and I can't believe my eyes but I believe my feelings. These women are radiating so much beauty, never have I seen and experienced anything like that in my life. What makes these women so beautiful to me is their determination to uphold their values, to resist violence...

Report from the fields.
Žodzina, 8.09

In a day, judges from the district courts of the Minsk voblasc heard all the cases (about 200). Some received warnings (girls), others — fines (from 3 to 10 base amounts), others — a review of the case with a notice to appear in the district courts of the voblasc, but some were sentenced to administrative arrests (mostly up to 10 days).

People from the Akrescina detention centre have also been transported to Žodzina to serve administrative arrests.

They don't beat people. All the boys and girls are fine. I want to thank the employees of the Žodzina temporary detention centre. They helped as much as they could with information and made concessions.

And many thanks to the people who helped with transport, brought hot drinks and cookies. For the general atmosphere of support and solidarity.

All the lists are on the channel: https://t.me/spiski_okrestina (the latest with the sentence length and dates of release).

Now something a bit more lyrical.
I felt that autumn had come 😒
Standing for 12 hours outdoors is an arguable pleasure.

And getting up at 6 am still isn't nice))

On 1 September, at the sight of a gang in black uniforms approaching us near the Red Church, we don't run away but lock arms with each other to form several circles, like petals of a rose, wrapping tightly, hiding the boys in the middle of the bud. We sing, and we sing, until the crows fly away.

📦 CARE PACKAGES REGIMEN

📍 Centre for Isolation of Offenders (CIO)
Minsk, 1st Akrescina Lane, 36
📞 (017) 372-73-80

Care packages regimen at the CIO:
daily 10:30 to 12:30

📍 Temporary detention facility (TDF)
Minsk, 1st Akrescina Lane, 36a
📞 +375 17 2394731, +375 17 3727411

Care packages regimen at the TDF:
daily 14.00 to 16.00

During the big women's march in the centre of Minsk on 5 September, I'm drawn to the edge of the column, closer to the road: there, older women talk to the siłaviki 'accompanying' us. Suddenly, I find myself standing in front of one of the OMON officers, shouting, "You betrayed us! How could you? You must protect us!" Shouting to the other women who scattered at the sight of a police van driving towards us, "No running, stand together!"

📦 CARE PACKAGES REGIMEN

📍 CIO on the territory of Žodzina District Department of Internal Affairs
Žodzina, Savieckaja St, 21 (Žodzina Territorial Centre for Social Services)

Care packages regimen on Wednesdays from 9:00 to 16:00 (lunch break 13:00 to 14:00)

On the evening of 8 September, participants of the rally in support of Maryia Kalesnikava were detained near the Kamaroŭka market, as well as on Mašerava Avenue in Minsk. We publish the list of detainees:

1. ▇▇▇ Viachaslau
2. ▇▇▇ Alena
3. ▇▇▇ Mauliuda
4. ▇▇▇ Palina
5. ▇▇▇ Sviatlana
6. ▇▇▇ Alena
7. ▇▇▇ Tatsiana
8. ▇▇▇ Uladzimir
9. ▇▇▇ Julija
10. ▇▇▇ Viktoryja
11. ▇▇▇ Fiodar
12. ▇▇▇ Siarhiej
13. ▇▇▇ Aliaksej
14. ▇▇▇ Kiryl
15. ▇▇▇ Katsiaryna
16. ▇▇▇ Ivan
17. ▇▇▇ Dzmitry
18. ▇▇▇ Pavel
19. ▇▇▇
20. ▇▇▇ Philip
21. ▇▇▇ Illia
22. ▇▇▇ Darja
23. ▇▇▇ Valiantsin
24. ▇▇▇ Maksim
25. ▇▇▇ Mikita
26. ▇▇▇
27. ▇▇▇ Hanna
28. ▇▇▇ Dzmitry
29. ▇▇▇ A.
30. ▇▇▇ Elina
31. ▇▇▇ Jury
32. ▇▇▇ Dzmitry
33. ▇▇▇ Aliaksandr
34. ▇▇▇ Faina
35. ▇▇▇ Hanna
36. ▇▇▇ Siarhej
37. ▇▇▇ Katsiaryna
38. ▇▇▇ Natallia
39. ▇▇▇ Aleh
40. ▇▇▇ Aliaksej
41. ▇▇▇ Alina
42. ▇▇▇ Anastasija
43. ▇▇▇ Ksenija
44. ▇▇▇ Palina
45. ▇▇▇ Uladz
46. ▇▇▇ Anton
47. ▇▇▇ Yauhien
48. ▇▇▇ Aliaksej
49. ▇▇▇ V.
50. ▇▇▇ Halina
51. ▇▇▇ Y.
52. ▇▇▇ Aksana
53. ▇▇▇ Dzmitry
54. ▇▇▇ Aliaksej
55. ▇▇▇ Illia
56. ▇▇▇ Siarzhuk
57. ▇▇▇ Kiryl
58. ▇▇▇ Aliaksandr
59. ▇▇▇ Yauhien
60. ▇▇▇ Vital
61. ▇▇▇ Inha
62. ▇▇▇ Ihar
63. ▇▇▇ Pavel
64. ▇▇▇ Illia
65. ▇▇▇ Alena
66. ▇▇▇ Natallia
67. ▇▇▇ Natallia
68. ▇▇▇ Mikita

69. ███████ Ivan
70. █████████ Anastasija
71. ███████ Ivan
72. ███████ Vadzim
73. ███████ Ivan
74. ███████ Dzianis
75. ███████ Natallia
76. █████████ Aliaksandr
77. █████ A.
78. █████████ Aliaksandra
79. ███████ Vital
80. █████████ Uladzimir
81. ███████ O.
82. ███████ Andrej
83. ███████ Anatol
84. █████ Andrej
85. ███████ Ivan
86. ███████ Mikhail
87. ███████ Kiryl
88. ███████ Yauhien
89. ███████ Mikita
90. █████████ N.
91. ███████ Yana
92. █████████ Alena Aliaksejeuna, born 1957
93. ██████ Katsiaryna
94. █████████ Mikalaj
95. ████ Aleh
96. ███ I.
97. ██████ Dzmitry
98. ███████ Radzivon
99. ███████ Andrej
100. █████████ Yauhien
101. ████ Anton
102. █████████ Stsiapan
103. ██████ Mikhail
104. ██████ Dzmitry
105. █████████ Aleh
106. ██████ Palina
107. ███████ Hienryjieta
108. ██████ A.

— What helped you survive through the imprisonment?
— I knew for sure that it'll be over.
And the girls, of course...

on the sixth of september we had a discussion about maryia kalesnikava   a couple of people supported a conspiracy theory that she was a russian stooge because the police weren't touching her   and I argued that she was one of us   they just decided not to take her for now and she would likely be arrested. so the next day I woke up and the first thing I read was that maryia kalesnikava had been detained   I thought that I had to mind what I say. it was a shock   because at that moment maryia kalesnikava was something so close to us   because   she appeared at different sites of the protest and although not for long   but somehow she was always around and it felt like on the seventh of september everyone had to come out to support her but the seventh of september was an ordinary day of course we were upset   and when the following day a march in support of maryia kalesnikava was announced   we walked there in a happy mood...

Tuesday
8 September

Tuesday, 8 September

First, a protest demonstration was announced near the National Art Museum: women armed with red lipstick were going to knit white-red-white scarves on its steps. I thought: we will definitely be stitched up by the police there. After that, Kamaroŭka was announced as the meeting place, and a women's march was planned.

I don't remember how I was preparing that evening. If I considered the option not to go. Why I had those particular clothes on. If I hugged ▬▬▬ before leaving the apartment. I only remember that I was very tired and got ready quickly. In addition, I was expected to be in three different places at the same time.

Ask me why I went to Kamaroŭka, and I won't be able to answer. Not because I don't remember, but because I don't know. I didn't formulate a comprehensive explanation for myself. There was no need for it: I did what felt right.

in general I perceived the eighth of september rally as rather broader not just exclusively women's because it was an action of solidarity with maryia kalesnikava   and there were more men than usual at women's rallies clearly because everyone was impressed by her deed with the torn-up passport and such persistence   that's why I didn't really look at it exclusively as a women's action. but in general of course there were many women there   well after all there are always many girls and women at these protests   so I wouldn't say that I felt something extraordinary...

People were brutally detained on the still almost empty square in front of Kamaroŭka: women of all ages. I stood on the steps of the covered market thinking I needed to buy groceries for ▓▓▓▓ and take them to her since she can't leave the house. Instead I rushed to the women. A man I knew asked me not to go, and I replied that I had to.

"Anyone of yours there?" "They are all mine there."

personally I had no doubts about whether to go or not   maryia was always a symbol of our protest brave honest   uncompromising about what was happening she inspired and   accordingly   I couldn't but go to that protest although it was already scary because   that period of lull had passed when you could   just walk around the city safely in the crowd of hundreds of thousands of people   fearing nothing...

39

Tuesday, 8 September

Emotional memory is a slideshow: we pull away a woman who's been grabbed by men in green uniforms; I pick up a small but heavy bouquet from the ground and throw it at the back of the policeman who is pulling someone aggressively, it hits him, he turns around sharply with crazy eyes but doesn't find me; together with the other women, I shout at the deputy head of the ▓▓▓▓ District Police Department who's come to conduct a 'dialogue' with us. "Why hasn't your Investigative Committee started an investigation about my child?!" "Return our children!" "1"

in those   days there were a lot of demos there was a small rally near the osvod those poor   guys who saved the protesters and took them to the other side of the river   they were detained   so several people gathered to hang posters near the osvod and   I noticed one woman there and literally half an hour later   we met at kamaroŭka   I went out from kamaroŭka with some strong-smelling products   in bags   and I see this woman in white trousers being pulled upside down into the car   and she screams help. so they drag her away I linked my arms with whoever was around still holding those bags but by that time they'd already dragged away several people and didn't pull out anyone else...

Finally I notice that there are a lot of us here. Shall I go to ▓▓▓▓ now? Or go to the station to see ▓▓▓▓ off. My gut tells me to go, it wants to protect me, but I merge with the flow and drown my guts out.

40

we saw police vans   they were circling all the time even by the   siluet shopping mall a lot of them but   they didn't touch us...

Tuesday, 8 September

we   crossed the road near kamaroŭka because cars had already started driving by and   it   was clear that using the underground passage   wasn't a good idea and even then you could already sense some tension   and by the time we started walking along   kujbyšava street some of the people   began to leave...

Right now, here, I can turn around and go to ▇▇▇▇, I promised her. It's my last chance. But I lack willpower to leave the crowd... This intoxicating feeling of unity and victory over fear...

I think back then it was a moment of thaw and well it seemed that the situation wasn't very dangerous it seemed that we could get away with it and though there was a feeling that something might happen we could have still gotten away with it...

41

Tuesday, 8 September

Along the way, I meet some people I know and I stop following what's happening around. How, my god, how can you forget about the danger when half an hour ago you were pulling people away from the police? Those 'walks' were a place of strength for us, so we didn't want to think about the worst.

initially we planned to go to vaładarka where according to someone's information maryia kalesnikava was but when we reached the intersection of kujbyšava street and mašerava avenue someone started saying that further along kujbyšava there were already police minivans waiting for us so everyone who crossed the road turned and walked beside the wall down mašerava...

Tuesday, 8 September

we were already walking along kujbyšava and were heading towards the niamiha   when suddenly someone screamed desperately that we were walking into a trap and that we had to go towards the avenue   so we all turned around again and went towards mašerava. well in fact there were probably traps everywhere that day...

before we even got to   mašerava we'd realised that there were provocateurs among us. we were led   somewhere not where we needed to go   we took some strange turns   and   basically when we found ourselves trapped   well I personally was not surprised...

so when we came to   that intersection   we walked further down and it was at that moment that   the police vans began to approach I   don't remember from which direction but   we decided to keep walking anyway...

why did we need to go there if there was a wall   I still don't understand how should I jump over the wall how should I run away?

43

Tuesday, 8 September

On the left, there is a road and police vans.

To the right there are fir trees. I decide that the trees will protect us and I start to retreat behind them, to the wall, dragging someone else along, maybe it was ███████.

we'd just come to the building we walked straight on and a car drove past and police started getting out they just encircled us and blocked us in and that's it and they ran towards us. first they blocked us in and then more of them were coming more and more and it was getting more and more frightening...

I remember that till the last moment I hoped that they would pass by because before that it was always like this with us that I walk and they either stop and intimidate us and we run away or they just drive by everyone gets tense but nothing happens. I really hoped until the last moment that they'd just pass by leave that they would scare us a little and leave but no way they got out and there are more and more of them and they're like hawks...

Tuesday, 8 September

I was focused on the conversation on some positive wave and indeed at some point I realised that we were surrounded I took out my phone called my husband and said that most likely I would be detained...

I turn around and they sh-sh-sh-oot past us I feel jittery we all rush towards the wall we stand against the wall hide the men behind our backs quickly hide behind us we link arms and they stand right in front of us we were in the first row...

I remember quite cinematically how we linked arms and were turning around to the wall because how we walked it was very strange that we were on the sidewalk and the wall it was further away and I remember that because I was under the fir trees and the fir trees pulled out my hair well of course if you move backwards oof like your shower and I remember very well how I noticed you in front of me and thought how I'll tell you about all this later and we'll laugh. I just couldn't reach you because there was a guy between us who you and I were protecting. and I wished you'd known that I'm standing behind you...

45

Tuesday, 8 September

We were surrounded and pressed against the wall. Our linked arms were easy to break, they didn't become our protection but remained a metaphor of resistance. What if we didn't want to defend ourselves? We wanted to not have to defend ourselves, to not be threatened. We wanted those people to go away and leave us alone. It wasn't even linked arms anymore; we just hugged each other as hard as we could, to protect.

We stopped being water, but we weren't giving up.

I was scared   my heart was trembling. when I stood arms linked and that green man in olive uniform tried to take me   the strongest impression was when I saw those hands in leather gloves on me it's like the materialisation of a picture or a film I mean you've seen this many times for example in the media and suddenly at some point you see this hand or this person so depersonalised suddenly you see it on your body and it left the strongest impression on me   just like a picture has come to life   I'm here this is happening to me now and I don't know how to get out of this situation. I realised that everyone was linking their arms   and I also tried   I tried not to be in the first row I think...

if not linking arms then what? there are simply no other options   and you know that   if they want it won't work. you deny it till the last moment that   they'll detain you now well because at first they didn't detain us they just stood there watching   and then when they started pulling us out   that's when it became   frightening because you see that   there's no chance that   the person next to you will not be detained...

46

personally I got pretty terrified when the cars pulled up I had a child left at home and so my goal for sure was to return home in the end but at the same time I was in no hurry to leave because my female friends were with me and well I felt responsible for them too. we pressed ourselves against the wall and linked arms...

I was a bit concerned about the others for example there was a woman next to me a bit older I was worried about other women another one had a pram I saw later that she was allowed to leave somehow it calmed me and as for us well they didn't beat us really they just pulled us from our linked arms forcefully...

I went to many marches with my daughter because I just didn't have anyone to leave her with. as we walked to kamaroŭka she fell asleep and slept through it peacefully in the pram so her experience was fine she wasn't aware of what was happening. I regretted bringing her with me because I and another woman were with prams and we stood aside and when the women retreated trying to stand tighter linking arms so that there was less chance of being pulled out we with our prams were a little in the way although we were standing on the side but they tried to be careful with the prams and I realised that though I meant well it was not very good because the other women had to take care not to push the pram and when we were surrounded one of the officers in a balaklava nodded to the other woman with a pram to go first and then to me well so I left because I was really worried about my child I understood that if they started pushing hard the pram could overturn and anything could happen that's why I left although later I felt somehow embarrassed and ashamed that I left...

Collective hysteria. Enraged, trapped women,

we defended ourselves as best we could — by singing and screaming. We did everything that worked before.

we sang songs   sang kupalinka   then we screamed   we squealed I remember he's standing and he's looking at me saying like   you have a good voice   why do you need to squeal   and we go even louder...

I wasn't too scared   on the contrary it was even a little   funny when the girls were all squealing and someone was like go ahead girls should squeal the louder the more we will scare them with our squeals...

interestingly that squealing at high pitch   I realised that in a stressful situation and the situation was   stressful undoubtedly   all people behave in completely different ways I was numb I mean I was afraid like   silently   I mean I didn't scream and in general it's not typical for me to scream even when I take part in a rally I never shout anything I feel shy   I always walk calmly and   don't go out onto the road either for me it's like   a violation of the rules I can't do it   I have to force myself to shout something or go out onto the road not because I'm scared but simply because I'm so used to walking on the sidewalk. I really like it when someone sings but a song is something that flows when you   are more or less calm and when you are under terrible stress and at that moment I felt under terrible stress of course I   was just silent I just deleted the telegram   and called my husband and deleted the telegram that's all I had the time to do...

Tuesday, 8 September

> we heard this kind of   hellish   groan the girls were   screaming for various reasons in the first place to demoralise   siłaviki and I remembered my grandmother's words about how the village next to hers was burnt during the war and for several hours she heard a rumble   as if from underground the rumble of voices...

singing is like some kind of hypnosis really there's this feeling that while you sing they can't touch you because well you stand there singing kupalinka girls so beautifully and the brain just can't comprehend how you can   be detained in this situation well it's just complete madness and that's why it seems that while you are singing   you have like a halo   that protects you   and that as soon as you stop singing   cruel things will begin and so you sing and sing kupalinka a hundred times   and   you're afraid to stop...

49

Tuesday, 8 September

I sang too of course I sang kupalinka with everyone because I don't know someone started I picked it up and in such a stressful situation it actually calms you down   to some extent we were also swaying while singing   and in principle this is a common thing when you're frightened you sing to yourself or in some other way. and those chants and swaying   to some extent allowed one   to mentally prepare   that you could be detained...

according to my proprietary method   I was dressed as usual   just as if I was going to a photo shoot for Vogue

I had red lipstick on   a jacket   a red high neck top   brooches   a solid stick umbrella kind of   elegant and if anything I could poke someone with it. and the shoes   beautiful but comfortable   and here I am in this whole outfit   with my hair done   thinking that I need to go join you   because you wrote to me that you were there   I know that you are there and here I am with this umbrella like la-la-la   I'm walking and I hear   a wild   scream I don't even know how   to describe it   as if   I don't know people are being shot such a wild scream terrible and   I immediately thought of   the moment from the book the unwomanly face of war by alexievich where   she met a woman who was   like in some kind of camp   which was located at the intersection of mašerava and bahdanoviča   and she says I remember that there was a pillar   here and right in front of me   a woman's baby was taken away from her and was killed against this pillar   and this was that exact place. and I heard that scream well   it was like a flash then I remembered this story   and   kept walking   but still   I don't know what it is in a person when you are terrified but curious   you don't even go there to fight for justice or tell everyone what you think no you've got terrified already but since you're here   anyway you're curious what's happening there what is there uh what's...

I was the second in the police van and I guess that's why   it was incredibly terrifying   because of the unknown because the women's screams started and you   just have no idea what's happening outside   I mean are they being beaten   or shot or I don't know raped   you can't see what's out there you just hear loud   choral screams...

They just watched us for a while, then they wanted to take the men and then, when we didn't surrender the men, an order must have come to take us too, because we refused to leave.

I saw or heard before how women would encircle men or kind of step forward because it was still a period when girls were mostly not touched   so they really pushed all the boys men behind them and even in front of me there was a row of   women with linked arms and we were behind them pressed against the wall   shrinking to the ground   and the women were kind of protecting us with their linked arms...

for some reason detaining us took so so long they probably aimed to get the men only   and then everyone who was fucking with them   and we were among those who were fucking with them as far as I understood   and it was all so terribly long and anxious   and I felt awfully thirsty...

Tuesday, 8 September

Tuesday, 8 September

the people in green   are standing in front of us   and they want something from us   and on the opposite side of the avenue people are gathering   and we shout for help   but they can't do anything either because   more and more police vans were driving up   and   we were told several times that   we could leave but   they would take the men   and of course for sure   you can't agree to it   we didn't even   even consider that option it was some kind of unpronounced collective decision. I really don't know what it's based on   some kind of human feelings   a sense of   dignity…

the women tell me   to hide behind them I say no how can I   an officer hide   so my wife and I stood in front   and naturally the police immediately moved towards me   first   and threatened to use force and I say we aren't violating anything   we're walking in a peaceful march   we aren't chanting anything   yes   we've come out on a march in support of maryia kalesnikava why not   I have the right to do that I want to support her. it lasted literally for about a minute or two then they knock me off my feet   they just beat me and   drag me into this van   eight of them…

so it happened that   the police van stopped right in front of me   the girls immediately   linked arms right and they pushed me behind them   there was a wall   behind us well basically there was nowhere   to run and there was nowhere to escape   so the police officers approached and just said lads   come along   I didn't try to resist well I understood that there really were a lot of girls next to me at least I don't even remember men near me   and   I did understand that if they wanted to take me they would take me anyway so I didn't resist and just followed them…

I remember a very funny moment when they started pulling out guys from the crowd you immediately stood like I won't give him to you and I wrapped my arms around him I laughed when I realised my hand got in his pocket. it was so ridiculous so comical you know the cops are pushing on and I'm laughing because I'm fumbling in his pocket I remember how he was shivering he was really shivering shaking and I couldn't talk to him because first of all I didn't know him and secondly his girlfriend was standing next to us and I think it would have been quiet a story if I'd whispered something in his ear so I just held him tighter. of course I didn't manage to keep him...

Many of us could have left, retreated immediately, let the men go, whined to the siłaviki, raised our hands, saying, "well, okay, we understand, you are stronger, let us go and we'll leave." But none of those I spoke to later considered doing that.

when you stand with linked arms you feel how people how their hands shake then you stagger and then you stand up straight a woman a mature woman was next to me and she was shivering so much that it is transmitted to you but you can't shiver so you try to hold your arms as tightly as possible. you can't give in to this panic if someone's next to you say a girl stands next to me she's calm then I feel confidence from her and if I shiver I transfer my panic to another person...

Tuesday, 8 September

I don't remember how I ended up at the other end of the wall.

"Please don't, go away, leave us, don't touch us, please, please, please!"

"Dad, daddy, please calm down, please, it's ok, go to sleep, I'm begging you, please, dad, dad!" In Russian. The little me didn't speak Belarusian. I only had these words to protect my mother. And again, I only have these words,

"Don't touch, please, please, please, please !"

they threw me into this mini bus and we started talking I say guys what are you doing and they started brainwashing me like you organised these young kids don't you know how it is in europe how in spain people are killed they are shot do you see peaceful rallies there? they shoot right away. I say you're talking nonsense naturally they immediately got rude like we aren't going to talk to you shut your mouth you scum that kind of talk. what was strange is that they didn't have any identifying marks I mean they had their camouflage and suddenly the driver receives a call and he's like daughter hi sweetheart are you back from school? so you seem to be a good person too how can you not understand what's really happening I understand what's in your mind you have an order I was a military man too I understand that there is an order and you must carry it out but whether you will carry it out is the question whether your human conscience will allow you to do it or not and I think to myself well you have a family you're talking with your daughter and I have a family too only my wife has just come up to the police van crying I say dear don't worry it'll be alright we'll definitely win...

I remember that we had to constantly pick someone off the ground...

Tuesday, 8 September

On the left, women are falling, pulled apart, and they are dragging me down with them. I fall to the ground too. A policeman in an olive uniform to whom I whined a second ago, says, "Help the girl!" It worked! He believed that I was nice and good...

At some point, after a lot of fussing, crawling and whining, when I managed to get mum, who kept yelling at dad, to stop it, while my sister and I tried to calm him down, he agreed to go to sleep. With my small hand, I'd take his large palm and lead him to the foldable sofa that served (and still serves) as a bed for my parents. I would play with him for a while to make sure he was in a better mood or I would gently lay next to him on the blanket until he fell asleep. And only then we could have some peace, until the next time.

when they pulled you down and you fell   it was obvious that   finita la commedia   and   I   honestly remember so well the moment when you fell because ugh where are you going hanna. I remember your jacket 'cause it was eye-catching. I don't remember the others but I remember that they pulled down the entire row   and I remember that they started to chase the boys   further down the row...

a friend of mine stood at the edge I stood next to him and of course they wanted to take ▇▇▇ and of course they couldn't pull him out and began to pull me out because we stood really firm but I have to say that the particular person who was there he was not aggressive he didn't show any aggression at all I think that if he'd wanted to physically pull me or ▇▇▇ out he would have done it... I even thought at that moment when he tried to pull me by my arms that he seemed to be afraid of hurting me I had a strong feeling that he didn't want to hurt me at all and didn't want to really pull me out. it seemed to me that this was happening somehow without a spark and that particular guy he he did his job rather formally as if he didn't want to do what he was doing. this lasted maybe a few seconds and then ▇▇▇ who was standing next to me said that he would go and clearly they needed him and I and the other girls ran away. although the court later added several days to ▇▇▇ sentence for resisting during arrest he didn't resist. yes at that moment I felt terrified there was no anger or hatred. then everyone who was in that line of linked arms ran away... I felt terribly guilty because it was like this person suffered because of me but on the other hand I then told myself well it wasn't me who detained him it's those people they are directly to blame it's not me who's doing this it's not my fault but still I felt bad as if he'd gone instead of me...

Tuesday, 8 September

> When I fall, something inside me switches and I can't control myself at all.

I'm not seven years old, and this is not my dad.

> I don't have to pretend to be a nice and sweet girl anymore, we can talk as equals.

then you got up and started shouting in their faces   it was such an oooh moment. this guy has already been taken away and I find myself standing right in front of them I have nothing because the girls behind me have linked their arms again and I'm alone   and I watch you walking in front of them demanding your rights and I'm like hanna fucking hell get the fuck out of there. you're furious with them and I'm angry with you damn it what the heck are you getting yourself into...

They tell us to go, they let us go. But before I have time to think, I see ▮▮▮ and ▮▮▮▮ being dragged into the police van.

those fuckers came up and said give up the men we won't touch you we pressed the men against the wall we stood in the front rows tried not to give them up   but we realised that it was impossible when the police started pulling us out literally just like that one by one and throwing us aside at some point I was just horizontally in the air that is the girls were holding me by my arms from behind and those fuckers were pulling my legs and at some point my shoes just flew in different directions so I'm barefoot and they threw me to the side at that moment I remember how I kicked the fucker not on purpose of course it's just when you are in the air and you are being pulled in different directions you can't really control it. and he said something to me like why are you kicking well he was even kind of offended he said it in a kind of childish voice I'm like dude how about asking yourself what are you doing? well I didn't tell him that   I thought it. after being thrown aside I put on my shoes and linked arms again and at some point   I saw that ▮▮▮ had been thrown aside...

I rushed after ▇▇▇ and then those dudes probably ran out of patience because they changed their minds about somehow throwing me aside but they grabbed us and dragged us into the police van and I think that plain-clothed guy said something like fuck you go ride in the police van something like this...

How can I leave now? My friends have been taken away, and I'll just go? All this injustice, which has been accumulating for weeks, I'm getting carried away. I shout to the men in uniform right in their faces, "You're violating our rights! We have the right to freedom of peaceful assembly and freedom of expression!" But they don't react, maybe because it lasts no more than half a minute, maybe because it doesn't bother them at all.

no way was I calm there was a moment when I realised that ▇▇▇ would definitely be detained and at that moment I started screaming and crying and I lost control completely I'm afraid to think what I could have done in that situation you know. so ▇▇▇ starts running they immediately grab him and I well we'd discussed beforehand that if he was detained I wouldn't follow him but at the moment when this happens you already kind of have only one right option so they grabbed him and I jumped on him and started screaming that I wouldn't let him go so they knocked us down together then they separated us and put us on our knees and wrung our arms a little. then they take ▇▇▇ away and they tell me like take your things and get out but I can't go anywhere anymore I'm running after him the guy stops me and I didn't understand at that moment why he was stopping me like it seems so obvious when my beloved is taken right there what do you mean I shouldn't go there should I just take my things and go home or what? for me it seemed so absurd that he didn't understand me and then another guy came up there was that furious bull and he was like well then you'll follow him...

Tuesday, 8 September

Tuesday, 8 September

gradually girls were taken away and I still didn't believe it I thought well no they couldn't a whole police van of women no way it's just beyond the pale but they actually took us they pulled me and they would definitely take my sister anyway and that's why the two of us went to the police van holding hands and that's it I mean they didn't use physical force they told us not to resist and they wouldn't beat us if we gave in voluntarily so we went to the police van ourselves…

I was detained because of the flag literally I was wrapped in the flag one guy looked at me with these inhuman eyes like take it off but I actually didn't hear it I read his lips and I was like I don't understand what you're talking about he doesn't mean me apparently it was some boss and he told some boys to take me there are two types of riot policemen those who really look at you with hatred as if you weren't a human and boys who have fun so to speak that is they really giggle while they do all this like a-ha-ha-ha we detained a bunch of girls such fun. it's not like I see this gaze at night but I remember it very well no one's looked at me like that in my life. two guys just came up and took me away…

there was a woman with a slightly older boy she tells him that he should see what he shouldn't become. we simply couldn't sit at home when there was no one to leave the children with it was out of hopelessness not because we are hiding behind them or as if we didn't care for them but simply when you read the news and your hair starts to move on your head you realise that you should be on the streets and you can only go with a child…

60

I don't know where people   run away
and scatter but there just ˙comes
a moment when there are many
many of us and suddenly you look
around   and there are about ten of
you left   and you don't understand
where the other people are...

so I saw this girl on a bicycle with a white helmet   and
a second later   she just looked like some kind of valkyrie
she really looked like she was in a movie these army men ran
out like all scary in their mossy uniforms   with balaklavas
and some women linked their arms   I found myself on
the edge of that raw   and that girl in her white   my god
helmet   she's like jackie chan she is so she got into a pose
she was ready to fight   she shrunk her shoulders   like hop
and   she's jumping like I'll fight back if something. that's it
and these   guys   or what to call them these military men
they started to take the men slowly the women started
screaming of course like what are you doing as always it
happens   and   an older woman   approached one of
the riot policemen or what to call them they were already
closing the entrance to the yard   so that no one would
come out from there   she approached him and said who
are you anyway that you are behaving like this here? and
he says come on I'm one of yours   we're good guys   and
with such a smile   and   it wasn't kind   it was like   I'll fuck
you up anyway whether you want it or not I'll fuck you up
and she was   an elderly woman...

Tuesday, 8 September

"You violate our rights! We have the right to freedom of assembly and freedom of speech!"

"I'm fucking fed up with you",

a bull in a black uniform, eyes filled with blood, grabs me by my elbow and leads me to the police van.

it was september after all   and it was clear they won't beat us badly   as if it was a period of a silent armistice of a kind   of course they were already starting to become more brutal again   and snatch people   but on the other hand they hadn't returned   to extreme violence   yet...

there were a lot of men already in the police van squatting when I was thrown right on top of them. I was the first female in the police van apparently before that they only took men and at some point they decided apparently enough was enough and started grabbing everyone because after me they filled the police van full of girls and women. so we sat there for 10-15 minutes and there were about 60 people packed in there maybe more and someone was fainting so we tried opening the windows.

Tuesday, 8 September

the officer who received us   in the police van   he constantly looked out the window and   laughed at what was happening   so it was funny for him   he spoke very unflattering words about the girls and women   about their intellectual abilities. he called them stupid wet cunts. in the beginning   there were somehow more young people   then they started getting pensioners in the end and older men too   the young people tried to get rid of their flags   and white and red bracelets   because they knew that those would make it worse   if found…

> my biggest concern when detentions happen is   always a flag to make sure they don't take the flag   it's like losing the banner of a regiment   that's why it's always vital for me to preserve it say when we were on the minibus   they tried to take the flags from us   they were snatching them from my sister and me and we didn't give the flags away   he just snatches it from you   and you hold it by the other end   and   pull it towards you and in the end   what I liked   they saw the resistance in it and stopped pulling it   but it's true that after that the bones of my hands   ached and it felt like there were bruises too just from the tension…

at the first moment I burst into tears   I was kind of hysterical I   didn't really cry because they took me but because of everything that was happening. in the police van   I cried a bit more   and a kind woman   calmed me down   she calmed me down   and that's it   later I perceived it as I don't even know how to explain it   not as an adventure but as   some kind of   experience…

63

I started having a panic attack

I started choking and crying but it continued roughly until a girl was thrown into our gazelle she was in an even worse condition than me and it works for me that only one person panics so if it's not me that means I stop so I was calming her down I'd calmed down myself and that's it and then I somehow managed to relax…

Tuesday, 8 September

and the next scene is one of the men shouted to them something like die you fuckers well you can imagine the policemen immediately got an adrenaline rush to their heads and a chase began there in that yard they ran after the guy and caught him in the end but along the way they hit an old man he accidentally fell something happened there and in the end they took that old man by his arms and legs literally and took him into a minibus without his hat barefoot because I don't know how this happened maybe they took off his shoes on purpose but he was toothless over seventy years old they took him by his arms by his legs and the most terrible scene that I saw during those events was they deliberately hit his head on a pole well it was intentional just like that bam and they carried him away I don't know why this happens why they do it and how I don't understand…

our stance was not to run away that is we aren't violating anything we have the right to peacefully express our civil stance we aren't criminals…

I didn't see the moment of your detention   and then they   offered a humanitarian corridor   so to speak   before gubopik arrived and there was a moment like   you know we don't trust them because who knows what they'll do if we move   and here they are standing silently and looking at us they look and we stand silently looking at them and it was like you know like   sheep in a wolf's trap   although I didn't want to feel that way at all but   that's roughly how it is and   I also remember that in the beginning there was a woman   with a little girl   next to me right against the wall   naturally the girl started to cry   and she was squeezed so hard that there was no space for her and no air and   she cried and said mum mum it hurts and   her mother couldn't do anything she was squeezed and she couldn't move and I was stroking the girl   to calm her and   I had to also   persuade the mother to   take the child out of there   and   to push a way   through the linked   arms so that they could at least   somehow pass and I stood and thought when we sang kupalinka   how traumatised the girl would be. ▇▇▇ was the first to walk through   that humanitarian corridor   in the sense that some girls had already gone ▇▇▇ saw that they were safe   she hesitated for a while but   still   she went   and I stood there and thought that   it was some kind of   betrayal that people are staying here and I will   leave. I thought about you   and because I didn't notice you I thought that you'd left already   so I went too…

Tuesday, 8 September

It's stuffy but not frightening in the police van. It's almost full, but we aren't going. I text ▇▇▇ that I was detained. I feel bad that I let down three people who were waiting for me, and I can't think about anything else.

I let my mother know from the police van I said that I'd been detained my mother was very   surprised and   she thought that I was joking   she knew that I went to the protests but   it was just very unexpected so when I told her she got very worried…

65

Tuesday, 8 September

as soon as we were thrown into the
minibus   a man was thrown on the floor
and my sister and I on the seat. what
struck me was that   my sister is fragile
and I'm not so big either but they used
a chokehold on us   the siłaviki put their
knee on both her throat and mine. it's very
difficult to describe   they throw you onto the
seats and   then they also press their knee on
your throat to immobilise you as I understand it.
I remember a thought flashed through my mind
right away a comparison with floyd yes I thought
well of course all of america stood up but here
you'll just get strangled and maybe no one will
even know about it. and   I also thought that of
course the lads didn't measure their strength for
them we are frightful criminals and it doesn't matter
to them who is in front of them   a child   an elderly
person   a woman for example   their task is to disarm
you. that hold didn't last long   we didn't suffocate   but
I know that my sister began to say something   she was
afraid that they would beat our friend and suddenly I hear
them slapping her   on the face very hard   and   then again
they hit her twice   but I was completely silent and he just
hit me. it was a very strong slap in the face   and again   for
him it was a slap   but for me   well it's just when I close my
eyes I see fire   all over my face   and I felt like my head was
about to fall off. I had a red mark   a red stripe in this place then
it hurt   for a long time. by the way until that moment I'd always
thought I was so proud   if god forbid I was ever hit by a man then
I just don't know I'd die. and you know what   nothing   no effect
no psychological trauma and by the way   after that I didn't start
treating men badly   I just now very clearly distinguish that there
are men   and there are people who currently serve in some kind of
security services   and for me they are not men...

and in the middle of those events I heard that scream again

probably it's when that famous shot was taken   when women are all pressed against the wall   and then I realized that's it   you're there   you're fine already you're packed there and sitting in that safe cap or whatever it's called   you've been disarmed you terrorist and will definitely not harm anyone   thank god the state is safe   because you are locked up. and I thought I'll call you   there was still connection   I dialed and naturally you don't pick up and you don't pick up   and you don't pick up then I get through   and I asked where are you and you're like I can't speak   I'm in a police van that was the last thing I heard   and the first thought was alright can't you run away   because I saw videos of how people could somehow slip out and run away so I thought let me go and hang out by the police van maybe you really decide to run away   so I went in that direction   and the next moment a minibus stops again and all these   green   olives run out of it   and I really thought well right now they will disarm me too   and for sure there will be no threat to Belarus   so   I'm standing like this   with my umbrella   and they just run past me like bullets no one touches me   and I just stand there beautifully   I had a feeling that I was probably already dead or why no one noticed me they didn't touch me they didn't take me and didn't talk to me they didn't even look at me…

Tuesday, 8 September

two security officers started moving towards us and a big guy moved towards me   I'm tall myself I'm one metre seventy-six centimetres tall he was taller than me a hulk and he walked with a very impudent grin towards me. he came up to me with his assured grin   pressed his entire weight on my hands and   they unclenched of course and at that moment   someone   pulled me from behind by my backpack   and several rows of girls fell and I also fell to the ground. I found myself lying on the ground   and   the security forces tried to pick me up from the ground and carry me   into the minibus. I actually remember all this quite vaguely   because a fairly large number of people gathered around me   someone was pulling me   several security officers tried to lift me some by my arm some by my leg   one tried to grab me by the neck. at first when I fell I shrank I thought they were going to beat me and I deliberately lay down in such a position that it would be impossible to hit me on the head I covered it with my hands and pressed my knees a little so that it would be impossible to hit me on my stomach. but   fortunately even at that moment they didn't beat or those particular security forces didn't beat women so   when I realised that they would not beat me   I   took a different position   you see about twenty years ago I did judo   and I did it professionally so   at that moment   although I didn't think that this would happen   my body remembered everything and   the security forces didn't behave very professionally they pulled me from both sides and using the strength of one security officer I pulled out my limbs from the other that is one pulls my hand and I pull out my leg   and when one security officer tried to grab me by the neck I simply moved away from the hold because that's what we were taught. at some point they   lifted me into the air but couldn't hold me   and dropped me   and I must say that all this time I was screaming so loudly that in response to those screams   a woman of about eighty ran out of the block of flats   and she also began to help fight them off. after fussing with me for about five minutes they simply gave up on me and left   I   didn't immediately understand   what happened and   for some time I probably just lay on the ground   until that woman came up to me   and said granddaughter get up quickly and leave before they take you. when I got up   there was no one there I found another friend   then several more minivans drove up and they ran to chase people around the yards   and we had to leave because it was clear that on the other side they were also packing the girls into the vans   and I went home...

My phone rings again, it's ▇▇▇▇, his coach is leaving for Czechia, and I'm in the police van instead of the bus station. I don't know when or if I'll see him again.

it's time to get on the bus   and you aren't there. I thought well   maybe you're just busy with your own business   maybe something happened or maybe you just can't make it   but when I called you in the end and you answered that you were sitting in a police van   it was especially   like I don't know   not tragic   probably tragic is not the right word   but of course it affected my emotional state in terms that   even before that I couldn't quite comprehend what was happening   at that moment I felt especially sad and lonely   I felt that   it was somehow wrong   that you were detained   and I was going somewhere...

The police van is packed, there are thirty-three of us in it, about twenty of them women. We're told that we're going to the ▇▇▇▇▇▇▇▇ Police Department. I hardly comprehend what is happening. Next to me are several elderly women and one with an icon, I've seen her before, on the first of September near Lanok. The women ask the two men in black uniforms accompanying us whether they believe in God... I'm sitting on a bench opposite the door, so I can see them very close, but their faces are covered, and I only remember how one of them had a moustache sticking out of his balaklava. The second one tells us proudly what a dedicated believer and Christian he is. How he goes to confession and communion, how he's going to the monastery in Lady for an important Orthodox holiday... The women and I look at each other, this is surreal.

what surprised me was that they tried communicating with us and that communication was very strange they could yell and their yelling was wild then they would switch to flirting and it was all so sudden flirting yelling flirting yelling no middle ground. I mean we tried talking about the political situation about the elections they tried to convert us there was even a moment when we said you're in balaklavas you're criminals that's why you wear them and so we drove them to such a state that one of them just like tore his balaklava off pretentiously and the second one too and the second one did it really funnily he wanted it to be pretentious but he tore it off and pulled it over his head you know like a gopnik really such a gopnik and he's so small and his voice is disgustingly squeaky and this balaklava I'm sitting and I think jeez this is hilarious they detained us they beat us but this is so funny and absurd...

"Anyone have water" "Here is some water, I prepared it specially for you..." says a policeman.

Drinking it seems dangerous and unpleasant, but someone does, because there are no options.

there was an older woman in our police van she was just telling them off it was pointless they didn't hear her anyway and they didn't change their opinion but she got herself into a state so her blood pressure soared. they got some water there was one bottle of water for everyone and say like aren't you afraid of covid? at that moment no one was thinking about covid or anything we all drank from the same bottle they even poured more water into that bottle for us someone joked that it's poisoned they're like it's not poisoned we drink it ourselves...

The one with the moustache sticking out from his balaklava asks, "What book did you last read?" He says this in all seriousness, with a sense of intellectual and any other superiority. Fuck, all the titles of the books that I have read or started, which lie on my desk, flew out of my mind. On the desk in my little room, which feel so unreal as if I've been in this police van all my life.

Tuesday, 8 September

there was also a moment they asked us if we had any piercing or cutting objects   and they asked it like shouting I'd say like   any piercing or cutting objects?! I say no and my sister says I have a nail file   and I think to myself now he's going to yell   but he's looking and smiling   well a girl always remains a girl he says   honestly it surprised me so much either yelling or flirting   and they very quickly move from one state to the other   this just shows their extreme volatility   and by the way you could see their eyes   many people talk about it that they are wild it's really like these eyes they're shifty eyes   they don't keep their gaze on you for too long   and they are so   so restless…

I noticed that the main guy in the police van   had a specific accent but mostly understood the belarusian language because there was an old woman   who was   swearing at them as much as she could and she spoke only belarusian   saying that someone will   fly on his golden plane and they will run after him on foot   and something else like this they   kind of laughed you could tell that he mostly understood belarusian but when he spoke   he had a specific accent which I as a philologist identified as ukrainian   right away   and later I realised the manager of our police van was a former berkut member   with a certainty of ninety-nine percent. but at the same moment he was kind of in a good mood   there were two women   who were coming from the opera house from work   one of them had a birthday and the next day a performance   he said in a cheerful voice   we bring our congratulations from   the minsk district police department something like that and then suddenly   when one of the men joked to him in response he cut him off sharply and rudely and   used foul language…

71

Tuesday, 8 September

I go up to the window to see where we are going, and just now I see that the glass is darkened, and we are like in a darkroom for developing film, and behind the window there is a photo that is being developed… I take out my phone and want to take a video of it. In Minsk in August, a Polish film maker was filming me for a documentary about our events, and he asked me to collect interesting footage to include in the film later. I thought that there was a perfect shot for a movie (no joking) and began to explain to our 'escort' that it was for a movie… A woman next to me was surprised and asked me how old I was. The one with the icon accuses me of being a show-off who protests insincerely… I don't understand what nonsense I'm saying and why I just won't shut up…

at first I didn't take it very seriously at all well because there were girls nearby and again everyone says that when you're around super cool people you giggle and don't take it all too seriously well firstly because it's absurd how can you detain me for me it's complete absurdity…

One of the detainees approaches the policeman standing by the door of the police van and whispers something to him. After that he tells her, "Okay, I remember you, we'll let you go." We hear it and look up at her — she offers us patties from a paper bag…

I wouldn't say that they behaved in any aggressive way no they behaved quite normally and they were like no worries we'll take you to the police department and they'll let you go it's all good don't worry they'll give you a telling off and you'll go home and we're like sure let's hope…

I also believed it and even bet an expensive bottle of wine…

I remember that in the end one of them began to tell us like with your protests all you'll achieve is that it will soon be russia here and then we'll see but in fact you're just so stupid you don't understand this in order to understand this you need to have intellect and I say to him exactly an intellect that you don't have and at this moment I see him rushing to me and just in that moment we arrive at the police department the doors open I was so happy that we stopped and there was the police department…

Tuesday, 8 September

there were already quite a lot of people   in the police van. there were two men who asked a lot of questions and when we arrived at the ▮▮▮▮ district police department we all got out of the police van and the two were told to stay. we were   already lined up along the walls in the police department   and after a while those people come in   and you could see   from their faces well they didn't have black eyes but the redness   as if they had been punched...

so I   reached   the intersection of   maserava and kujbyšava   and it took me probably four attempts   to unlock my phone because my hands were shaking   but they were probably shaking you know this state I was in a frenzy   I was leaving the site I was   cursing probably like you into their faces but   to myself. I found ▮▮▮▮ she was waiting for me and we   decided that we needed a drink   and we went   to some georgian restaurant   I remember very well that I immediately ordered a pint of beer   and a massive steak to make up for what's happened and   I open facebook and see under my post that they detained ▮▮▮▮ that you were detained too. to say that I was angry is to say nothing because   every time we met   I could see that you were drawn to these battles and you just wanted to be detained. that's why   I wasn't surprised   but I was angry because fuck   she finally got it   and here they bring me my steak   and I have this pleasantly cold glass of beer you know   and I clearly remember that I   decided that I'm not going anywhere I will not leave until I eat this steak and drink this beer...

I was supposed to go there too but I was called to work   I sat at work and followed what was happening via onliner and tut.by   and I looked for you in all the photos   you always wear a very bright jacket   'cause you're going to a rally of course you have to stand out. I came home from work   it was already eight in the evening   I check my telegram to see if you were online   you weren't. hanna komar last seen recently. I messaged you but you didn't reply   then I messaged you again   and I realise that I need to look for some of your friends   at that moment I didn't even think that you have a million friends and that everyone is already looking for you anyway and knows something   I think oh god she's there alone   what will happen to her   poor baby...

on that day I went to the theatre   with my friends for the first time in a very very very long time   it was jura divakou's performance of gogol   and the most interesting thing was that the performance was I think from two thousand   eighteen but it was all about belarus   we saw it in august and september   and it was so strange   and   it was frightening to be in the audience to watch it   and try to experience these feelings   and   when we left the theatre I found out that   you'd been detained   and it was   just madness because those were the first detentions since the beginning of august   well I mean massive ones   and it was horrible   and   well I also joined   the girls and we were calling   the police department we just couldn't understand   where you were   what was going to happen to you   because back then those were the very first days when   they started detaining women en masse   and it wasn't clear at all   what's going on where to call where to go and how to help   what can be done   although   to be honest   I was almost one hundred percent sure   that you would just be released maybe with fines   I couldn't wrap my head around the idea that   someone could be imprisoned   I just couldn't wrap my head around it at all on that day...

> I didn't follow the lists of detainees back then and what   I was in a panic   not that I was running around the flat but I had to do something   but   I had no idea what could be done. usually in life I imagine roughly what is happening where and how it can be influenced so that it goes in the right direction   but in this case it doesn't work and god knows what to do...

███ █████ and I called each other until the night   people were let out in batches   and   we were hoping that they'd let you out too   because some previous time   they also grabbed people and then all of them were released at night   without money   with dead phones or without phones because they were kind of put under arrest   and that's why the guys   decided to wait...

Tuesday, 8 September

I don't look at anyone and I don't memorise anything, I'm hiding somewhere in a corner inside myself. It all has just begun, and I already want to forget it. I hope, like all of us here, that we will be released after the reports are filed, although deep inside I know that I'll receive administrative arrest. We're brought into the police department training hall and told to turn off our phones and put things in front of us. Some have neither bags nor backpacks; their things — keys, money, phones — are placed in transparent files which are stapled together. They are lying on the floor like jellyfish bodies... A young cop with a fancy haircut mocks my Belarusian language.

I mock him back.

I mostly   understood the rules of the game   and already in the police department   when we were standing in the corridor   my task was to preserve myself   as much as possible   in order to get through it as unscathed as possible   because I didn't see the point of being obstinate at that moment in that place they had their system well established   they just they put you there and   you roll along it   as if on a conveyor belt   and so if you spread your arms wide they'll simply break off   during the ride   on this conveyor belt   so I squeezed tight as much as possible inside me   I concentrated and tucked myself up...

Tuesday, 8 September

we were brought to the ███████ district police department and they put us in a room the size of a classroom with chairs they   gave us water   and began asking our names   where we were registered   where we worked and so on. then they filmed us on the phone   like you turn around you say your name where you live   then there was some kind of questioning   it took ages   so the cops started getting into discussions with the detainees   and   I was dozing there on a chair and then   it became clear that it wasn't gonna end soon   dasha found a badge with pahonia in her pocket and was trying to figure out how to get rid of it   and in the end she threw it out in the toilet not to be charged with extremist activity...

We have our temperature measured. I have a high temperature. They say that everyone with a high temperature will definitely be released. I believe it and I don't, but I don't feel sick; probably my temperature rose from the stress.

I had a temperature of 37.6 probably   I didn't even think that I had it but when they measured it when we stood in that line   I was very surprised probably it was because of the worry but   they thought that it could be coronavirus   and then they put us   aside apart from everyone...

77

Tuesday, 8 September

I sincerely hoped that they'd let you go right away so I was just going to meet you. I didn't have anything with me   at first I didn't even know   where that police department   was. for some time   until ▮▮▮▮ and   all your friends arrived   I stood there alone and didn't know what to do and where to put myself   there were no lists of the detained   ▮▮▮▮ also called me all agitated and asked where to come   because back then for some reason we thought   that we were obliged to come and stand by the police department...

I   found out about your detention , in the evening   I was embroidering and preparing for a meeting with the neighbours and then I find out that you were detained   and I think I wrote to your sister first   but she didn't answer and   I learnt that the girls   were going to the police department so I decided that for now I'd go to the meeting   and then might go to the police department I had a nasty feeling that   no one would be released that day because from the pictures it looked absolutely horrible...

I was running a temperature from the stress...

78

Tuesday, 8 September

I'm one of the first to go to the investigator's office because of my temperature. The office of the investigator Makukh Andrey Aliaksandravich. From his walkie-talkie, I hear how the courtyards where people gather with their communities are patrolled. He calls what we do 'kindergarten', he also says he trusts the teachers at the school where his daughter went to the first form. He has two higher degrees, and he is trying to convince me that our white-red-white flag is fascist. He asks me, "Can you speak Russian?" He asks but doesn't force me, for which, according to his logic,

I must be grateful. As well as for the fact that we aren't beaten. And for being taken to the toilet.

we were   taken to the toilet we could   those who smoked were even offered a cigarette but   nevertheless I think that   even if they treated us ok   it's still not normal   because   it's in the order of things that they take you to the toilet or   allow you to smoke but for some reason from their side it was some kind of   mercy as if   look   we allow you aren't we great...

79

Tuesday, 8 September

the people who lived opposite the detention centre allowed us to use their toilet   they took out a table they brought hot water   so that people could warm themselves with tea or coffee   they brought some food to the people too…

of course there were fears   in the first place that you'll be hurt   physically because nothing is clear you know there's really no logic to it suddenly someone becomes an irritant for them   for example as we stood there everyone was treated more or less ok   and one guy just asked a question   when they were drawing up a report or something like that   and for that they spread eagled him   in this uncomfortable position and they beat his legs   they said something to another guy like we'll talk with you alone and they took him somewhere   so you don't know   at what moment what will annoy them in you   and you can become a victim of this harsher scenario and this uncertainty this lack of logic   say they didn't like someone and that's it   and this fear that it could be you   who will fall into a narrower   category   of people who get the worst treatment although of course if we are talking about reality which is normal   not distorted not twisted inside out then all this is horrible   it's a violation of rights   at every stage and so on…

we arrived at the police department   and there were already a lot of people like a party   lots of food   someone was constantly bringing sandwiches   coffee from mc-donald's   there were about six chargers   and tons of power banks   and people who lived in the houses nearby they would come and help. we didn't have any information we stood   waiting   and there were a lot of us   so we somehow held on because there were a lot of us waiting for you there. mutual support   made a difference…

I start looking for the paper slip with contacts that you pinned on your wall   I start   making calls   your sister your friends   they are like yeah we know she's been detained. I started   collecting things for you but I didn't know what you'd need there what you were wearing and I thought if I was there   what would I need and I started collecting things in my mind according to that list. it's such a responsibility you feel like pull yourself together   you can't   be upset and   you need to pull yourself together. I learned how to collect things quickly from this experience. and it was like   here we go the moment came when I was packing a care package   for someone   I took some things with me put the most necessary things into my backpack   and left for the police department…

> as soon as the information appeared people who know you started writing to the groups on facebook and instagram   asking if they could help somehow and if there was any more information   and what to do…

they showed I'd say   a good attitude towards us emphatically good   they didn't insult us   they had some conversations   of a quasi-political nature with us   of course   with a bias towards some kind of conspiracies that we were paid for protesting but of course it's all funny to listen to   and   when you look at them you get the feeling that some of them simply memorised the text it's even in their intonation   and they retell this text to you and you understand that there's no particular meaning there even if they repeat it a hundred times…

Tuesday, 8 September

Tuesday, 8 September

a young boy   a policeman   came out and was saying something to us that there would be lists of the detained later   and that's what he kept saying for three hours   or more. people tried to engage the boy   in a conversation saying how can you be here   are you on their side   don't you know what's happened there what events happened in august how can you work here   and he's like well I understand everything but also   I have my own opinion on this   you know I listened to different people   well he meant his bosses like   karpiankoŭ that kind of people and he's like of course I don't agree with them on some things   but in general   they are right and I'm just from that dialogue I simply   moved away because I understood that it was all pointless   but maybe it was right that people were trying to explain something to him and in general it was   ok   he really tried to listen to them   but of course they were so brainwashed   he just spoke in memorised phrases...

They were drawing up a report for a long time:

first they ran out of paper for the printer, then they forgot the computer password, then the printer didn't work, then they couldn't find the report form... About two days before that, I'd asked a friend to role-play a detention and interrogation with me so that I'd remember which laws to refer to, but we didn't have time, and now I don't know how to behave or what to say.

no one gave us any information   everyone was waiting for something exchanging lists of who where what and   there was a bit of   tension this feeling that   the detained are there behind the walls and you are standing here on the loose and you don't know what is happening with them there this kind of a restless feeling. some people were exchanging updates   who was in which police department because relatives and parents and   friends   were coming to find where people were because they didn't know...

at first we probably waited for two and a half hours for the lists   to confirm that you were there. the only thing I ate was one   sandwich   someone shared a blanket with me   but at two am they took it because people were leaving   and   I stood there freezing for three hours   well because I literally had nothing and   it was hard for me because   I have this   I don't know what kind of disease it is when I stay in the cold for a long time I start having   pains and I can't   lift my legs. so I stood there right to that point...

"I was walking around Victory Square and saw women pressed against the wall, they were frightened. I joined them in order to support them, because I was frightened myself..."

was recorded in my report.

Tuesday, 8 September

in the report in the end   they mainly   wrote the truth   well only the time was wrong   but it was written that I screamed   although on that day   I had a sore throat and I couldn't scream   that is at that moment   I didn't scream   I only remember how we sang kupalinka but because of my throat I couldn't sing   loudly   long live belarus I didn't chant it but they wrote that I   did   and that I didn't behave   very well. two hours I think it took them   too long for a report...

███████ police department   minus one star   out of ten. we sat there for maybe five hours   and nothing was happening and we weren't allowed to talk to each other   we weren't taken to the toilet except under escort   and even still we had to ask   and they did everything torturously slowly they didn't show me a single document. they had such bad processes that they   interrogated only two people   and for everyone else they wrote that we refused to testify   or that we don't trust the court something like that...

I was given two reports to sign one for the actual march and the other for resistance   although I actually didn't resist. when they gave me this second report   I realised that   I didn't want to sign anything at all   that is I already disagreed with both of them the officer told me that it wouldn't affect anything   and I could see that the investigator himself   somehow sympathised with us he understood everything but that's the situation he was in. I asked for copies of the reports and he made copies for me   but not everyone   received copies of their reports...

I   admitted that I was   on the march   if you consider it a march then yes   I was on the march   in support of maryia kalesnikava why can't I do it   I don't plead guilty I didn't hit   anyone I walked peacefully with my wife I talked with the other   normal people. I didn't sign anything...

84

I take dry and wet wipes, a bottle of water and a book with me from my backpack. "So you're prepared," the investigator shares his genius insight when I take the book. In fact, yes, I was prepared because sooner or later I would be detained, and just a few days before I read in one article that they were obliged to let me take the book with me.

there were also two women officers   who were   listing our possessions   and one may expect them to be   in solidarity with you   and they seem to be talking to you kindly   but   mockingly that's how it felt. they told us you won't be taken to prison   you don't need your things with you so the girls didn't take them and ended up in akrescina prison without the things they needed...

Tuesday, 8 September

I'm in the room where I'm photographed and where my fingers are 'rolled' with a black liquid that doesn't wash off well with cold water. The young man who takes pictures invites us sympathetically to treat ourselves to sweets and take more for others as well. "Will you send me the photos? For Instagram", I joke, feeling a sense of trust, having encountered a sensible, as it seems, person.

absolutely sensible they said they don't work here   they are like an operational group that was sent purely for all those procedures   that's how they positioned themselves that   they were like not with the police but they just were outsourced and here are candies girls enjoy   they were nice...

Later, when a nervous and angry guard in a balaklava comes out of the office, we actually look at my photos. I don't know yet that these people don't have the right to film and fingerprint me before I was sentenced. But they know... "My tattoo looks not bad in your photo," I joke, looking at a picture of the tattoo on my ankle. "He does everything that's below the waist well," replies the officer who took the fingerprints and with whom we discussed falsification in schools a couple of minutes ago... The woman with the icon is also here, bullying me and accusing me of insincerity.

Tuesday, 8 September

when I was having my belongings listed I was told to take my shoelaces out   there was a young   woman officer   sickishly sweetly polite   one man said to her like   why are you so happy and pleased is something cool happening here? she's like oh   so what should I be impolite? well it was really such a dissonance that we're all going to akrescina   with our whole damn cool party and here's this happy babe. she says to   me take your little shoelaces out please and I'm like am I going to a little jail? she's like that a-ha-ha-ha how did you say little jail oh-ho-ho-ho-ho-ho   I don't know what they're going to do with you   I say are you telling me they're going to let me out without my shoelaces   like do you need my shoelaces?..

then   already after drawing up the report   one policeman told the chief that   we have high temperatures we went to where the main entrance is and the policeman asked to call someone   upstairs whether to let us go or not because we might have coronavirus. but in the end when this security guard called   they said no   and that's it...

we were certain that the people who were detained the first time would be released that's why we waited   well we heard some stories that they could release people at two am and you'd stand there lost so we all waited   well or someone stayed on duty there. we waited until   the morning...

Tuesday, 8 September

My temperature is normal. I go back to the training hall and the same cop with a fancy haircut takes my shoelaces from me.
I understand that I'm here for a while, so I decide to treat the situation as a writer — to observe. I have an opportunity to see how it all works from the inside and tell about it.

in a sense I felt relieved because the unknown scares me the most in life imagination sometimes paints worse pictures than in reality so when I got there and found out what it was like it was easier for me to actually go out to the protest next time...

we were brought to the ▇▇▇▇▇▇▇ district police department and I saw the work of a police department for the first time. one may think that everything is so well structured there but from what I saw there's no system it seems like there's no communication between the police officers here they are sitting they are somehow calling who hasn't had their fingerprints taken yet? it's like they come to you and ask what to do they're lucky that belarusians are nice people because who didn't give their fingerprints the people don't hide I had the feeling that if it hadn't been for our help the police officers wouldn't have even figured out how to do it all. it felt like the policemen themselves were so used to all that they're just tired of everything these protesters because I know that even our belongings they documented each item slowly writing something looking at it and I watched it and it seemed to me that all that work could be done with proper organisation in an hour maximum and we were kept there for maybe five hours...

Tuesday, 8 September

around one am that young officer brought us a list of the names of those detained he managed to write down he read it out very quickly and sometimes he called some names incorrectly or there were no names and you didn't know for sure if that was your person so we just wrote down what he said to decipher it later and share with viasna and so several times he'd go back to ask the names or surnames and add people to that list then he'd come out to us again and read it out...

there was a sixty-five-year-old teacher with us and her blood sugar rose very high well of course we asked if there was a doctor but there wasn't and also a seventeen-year-old girl was sitting with us we refused to let her be interrogated and demanded they call her parents in the end the officers gave in and called the parents who came and took her away and the ambulance also came and took this woman with high blood sugar and took her away...

89

Tuesday, 8 September

the scariest moments were when the ambulance came twice well because we didn't know what they were doing with you there. the ambulances stood there for maybe forty minutes and you stand and pray for forty minutes hoping it wasn't hanna. well you know I probably needed that experience it's like you have friends and you take it for granted you somehow don't think about it you have them and they're cool and you never focus on what you feel and whether you feel anything at all in your daily routine. but at that moment I stood there and almost cried because I could not imagine that something would happen to you...

> an ambulance arrived at some point then it stopped and told us who was in it and to which hospital they were going. then police vans arrived. at some point we had to go to the car because it was cold and my feet were frozen I wrapped a sweater around them...

I remember how we huddled close to each other when it was cold it was very cold there and even more so when they forced us to take out our shoelaces which made it even colder... we were still wearing shoes at the time it was the beginning of september and already when we were at the police department my feet felt cold and I know that ▇▇▇▇ received socks she saw that I had bare feet and she gave me her socks it was somehow so touching because you see that a person has practically nothing but she shared that with you and instantly from strangers you become very close...

90

They're fine, they even want to order a pizza. That's how we knew you were hungry, and some parents begged the officers to take at least some food from what the volunteers had brought for you people there. But all our requests were crashing against the wall.

we had time to get to know each other we were exchanging experiences talked joked laughed and in front of us there sat three or four very grumpy policemen who looked like a pile of rubbish   and they looked at us   well I thought with envy because they were so bored…

There's a rolled-up volleyball net above the door leading out from the training hall into the corridor and you have to bend to avoid getting tangled in it, but everyone who walks through the door gets caught in it and has to disentangle themselves. I watch this movie for hours, I desperately want to write everything down, but there's no pen, and I try to memorise it, repeating, scrolling through the details in my mind many times.

I was trying to joke all the time offering them to stretch this net and play volleyball. we're sitting there it's impossible to sleep it's impossible to relax a cop stood in front of me I say let's stretch the net and play volleyball he looked at me with a twisted face no I say ugh you're boring. they were not prone to jokes they were all rather tense…

Tuesday, 8 September

to the right of the entrance   to the training hall   there was like an iconostasis   of the best policemen   well basically an honours board   for policemen   and above the entrance   right above the entrance there's an icon   I've never really seen anything like this literally an icon and to the right   the policemen. they also have an interesting knight   a little in the back of this hall.a medieval knight   well I guess he also symbolises a kind of knightly honour and nobility   inherent in a policeman   as policemen wish to believe...

and we noticed that   all the portraits and names of the employees were removed from the stands...

at the police station they kind of treated us ok   but it was disgusting when they brought us in and   one of the guys was like oh girl you should be going on dates and not to police stations   and I really   wanted to punch him...

Tuesday 8 September

"What a beautiful wedding we'd have: I'm in my uniform, you..."

the same young policeman with a fancy haircut is flirting with our girl. She answers him and smiles, I don't even listen anymore. Recently, a friend from Denmark told me about Danish women who got into relationships with the occupying soldiers during World War II...

a policeman was hitting on a girl sitting about three people away from us I remember this very well because for me it was kind of insane   how he said that he would save her or   I don't remember his exact words but my impression is that he said that he would save her but he couldn't do anything more or he could do something   but he didn't   just words   why what for   he says that he studied law   and I don't get it what kind of lawyer he could be   I couldn't understand how a fourth year student   thinks completely differently and understands I think he understood that we were brought there   for no reason   and yet   he was doing his job   he was doing it anyway...

Tuesday, 8 September

there were these two cops   who gave us information about the detainees. one a little dumb   with a camera   he was filming us everything we were saying and the other young man   was nicer you know not nasty it was ok to talk to him   but he argued with us a lot he was obviously bored you know it's more fun to talk to people   or debate   than just stand there. our discussions were just madness   his argument was that   the cops were beaten up   omon were beaten up they were so traumatised   poor things   and we are like do you even acknowledge that they detain women   like   how can they beat you up. in general he spoke in cliches   I even felt a bit sorry for him that he spoke with those cliches and   he was like I   never hit   anyone   anywhere. he told me I was a provocateur but I understand that he was also flirting a little   well you know   I'm a girl it was obvious that he was interested   plus I stood there for a long time…

while we were waiting a young cop   so he organised a kind of show like let's get married   he was trying to matchmake some young guys from the detainees and the girls so he was asking our zodiac signs   googling compatibility of zodiac signs   and telling us all this. well he was the most ok one and the best thing he did was he let us call from his phone because   our phones had been taken away back in the first police department and our relatives didn't know that we'd been transferred. actually   it was kind of entertaining I mean   the time passed quickly thanks to that   charade. we also tried to talk to him about serious things we asked him about his life why   he's in this system   he said that he's   an athlete he's been involved in sports since his youth   playing billiards   and he's been abroad twice to competitions and   in short everywhere is crap   we don't need this in our country…

personally I didn't like
that moment   at all
when he tried   matching
couples   it was so funny
for everyone but it just
made me   shudder
like   come on   how can
you talk with them at
all   why do you find it
funny   it really   irked me
like   they were trying to
befriend the enemy...

Tuesday, 8 September

                    the attitude towards girls and boys was different   for example   the boys could be spread eagled and growled at and were not allowed to sit or come to the window   but the girls could whisper among each other   and almost all the time there we sat on the chairs...

I remember that young   cop
how he said something   like
I don't care who'll talk to me from
the telly I don't care who's top dog
the main thing for me is that   I now
receive nine hundred rubles   that's
enough for me   but what will happen
in the future I don't know the main thing
for me is that my family is provided for and
I'm provided for   but as far as I understand he
doesn't have a family   yet he's still studying   he
studied   he was an intern...

a cop an old geezer   he was sitting there   then he's like oh girl   so how old are you? I say well   thirty he's like   and do you have a husband and children? I say like   no   so where do you work? I say well   in IT   so how much do you earn? I say a lot   oh goodness how so how has this happened I say well that's how it is old fellow   good morning. he was like   oh my god   of course   as if he sobered up to see the apocalypse...

95

Tuesday, 8 September

People leave and come back, there are more and more of them on our bench, and fewer and fewer on the opposite one. I try to read or sleep, no energy left for conversations.

those who had young children were released and one girl was just let go we were surprised...

we chatted all night through with the person sitting next to me he was a businessman who just came there out of curiosity to have a look. he simply got tired of reading telegram channels and he came to see how it all actually happens...

Tuesday, 8 September

we were all talking   all intelligent people   ninety-five percent of them with higher education all of them were sensible   and understood what was going on   and most importantly no one was in any kind of   negative mood everyone was confident in their rightness   and in their inner   spirit   as if charged with the energy   from all of the marches from   everything that had happened before...

the documenting process itself is also   well it's somehow   I don't know they were documenting me in the same room with a man who was very anxious   but I felt calm and funny and appalled because   the cop documenting me   was very   shady   I can find no other word for it he was lecturing me about my sister he was trying to pressure me and make me feel guilty   because my sister was detained   that it was my fault that I dragged her   and do I know how dangerous it is   like this and I need to mind my behaviour   well I tried to argue   but it was four in the morning   he was terribly tired I was too   and I   kind of said that yes I was at the rally   I don't deny it   and   I was sure that they would let us all go   because there were about   forty or thirty of us there all women and the thought that they would now take us to akrescina   seemed even more absurd to me but there was no limit to the absurdity...

At four in the morning, several officers start packing our things into boxes. Some of the detainees guess that we're going to Akrescina, but I refuse to accept it to the last.

Tuesday, 8 September

for some reason   I actually expected that they would let us go   judging by the stories that girls were usually let go and   considering that we literally did nothing like yeah   we just walked down the street   we didn't attack nothing like that   but I knew that they could anyway I mean I had a suspicion that they could   but still I was sure that   they wouldn't take us to prison   and therefore I was calm although when they started organising us in lines   and calling our names   surnames   and organising us close to the wall   it was surprising I can say   I was scared for two minutes   but then I got myself together and   everything was fine...

           as far as I understand
           it wasn't a decision
           specifically of those in
           the police department
           but an order from above
           because   when we went
           out to the toilet   there
           was a chief the chief from
           the police department
           the one who was okay
           he was on a call   and
           he was like what should
           I do with these? so
           everyone to akrescina?
           I heard that yes everyone
           to akrescina...

We're moved towards the wall, trying not to lose our shoes (without shoelaces) and we stand in four rows, back-to-back. They take us out and put us in an old bus. It has curtained windows and not enough seats, three people on each double sit...

98

and they drove us to akrescina...

I remember we passed my house since I lived nearby   and   I remember how I wished I'd been sleeping in my sweet bed...

when your bus   was leaving   I knew that it was your bus   because before that a police van had left exactly at one am. there remained three women   in the police department   and   the fucking officers refused to tell us the names of those   who remained. there was   a man next to me who was waiting for his wife   she was detained   and we   took   turns   peering into the windows trying to see something but I could see   nothing   we only saw a woman's silhouette and   wondered what was happening there and whether   that silhouette looked like you   or his wife...

Tuesday, 8 September

there were three of us women who had children so we were supposed to be released before midnight but the police pulled a trick on us I don't know if it was on purpose or out of stupidity in short they loaded our things with everyone else's and took them to akrescina. so when everyone else was taken away they told us well go home I said you're kidding me I didn't know then whether my husband knew or whether anyone would come for me I said I don't have any money a phone or a card are you suggesting that I leave at night like that? he was like well okay wait here while the car will take your bags and bring them back. we waited another hour pestered the officer on duty and finally he called akrescina and said no the car wasn't there yet and hadn't even unloaded yet so we decided to leave as we were. we went out and it turned out that our husbands were waiting for us they came for us. so they took us home... we were like oh what where are they taking them looks like they're transferring them we need to go. the bus was driving pretty fast   a couple of times it went through a red light   we weren't allowed though and we had to stop   it felt like the driver saw that we were following   and wanted to get away from us   but he couldn't. and also at some point   a motorcyclist was riding behind   following the bus too. a couple of times we thought that we had lost the bus but it had to stop at a traffic light I guess so we caught up with it because there was a green light for us. we arrived at akrescina and stopped somewhere there   the bus also stopped for a bit while they were opening the gates   we got out of the car and looked into the windows in case someone would look out   but you probably weren't allowed to look out although while we were driving someone in the back seat of the bus was apparently   trying to make us understand that yes yes   we are here. the bus drove in   the gates closed and well that was it...

we are riding in a police van   you're riding along the streets of minsk you imagine where you are roughly   and you have a feeling   as if you were saying goodbye for a while   to these streets   and to walks...

100

volunteers stayed by akrescina twenty-four hours   doing immense work sitting in the cold at night collecting information and updates. we approached them they told us which chats to join we joined every one of those they told us honestly the best thing you can do now is go home and sleep...

Tuesday, 8 September

I went home   and
I   lay down with my
son   and   I thought
god forbid that he ever
gets into such a situation
experiences some kind
of events that normal
peaceful people should
not experience   and
I thought what a blessing
that I'm now with him
that I'm at home that
I can hug him and I could
not get enough of him
and of my daughter too...

Tuesday, 8 September

all night I had nightmares that someone was breaking into my apartment and I couldn't come to my senses for a long time. before that I didn't need to   hang anything in my window but after what I saw on mašerava avenue   I needed to   get my stress out somehow I had white and red wool for knitting   and I wound a white red and white flag from the wool around the metal railings of my balcony. it was like meditation for me my anger powerlessness resentment some of them   subsided as I was wrapping the wool around those railings but still I slept badly I felt like barricading the door…

I returned home at five in the morning and   I was so cold that even though I really wanted to sleep I   took a bath and I couldn't get warmer for another forty minutes I think…

Finally, I saw Akrescina… White walls and wire, the sky is high, and we care about absolutely mundane things: who we'll get into the cell with. They let in three people at a time, we try to group so that we can be together, those who made friends at the police station and on the bus.

it was much easier for me because I was with you and I felt good but I couldn't understand what I was doing there it felt like I was in the wrong place and I didn't fully believe that I was there I don't know how to explain it it's just like I'm in some kind of haze and this is happening not to me but it's happening well somehow I'm participating but it's not me speaking and it's not me at all. I wasn't scared no I didn't have any fear I just don't even know I remember how we laughed at the whole situation I remember when they walked us all the girls near the building those white walls around on the street we just stood there and laughed at the whole situation…

they brought us it was dark they lined us up along the wall and we stood along the wall they were walking around documenting us you couldn't turn your head well first of all panic you're standing there and you don't know they're walking past you back and forth you don't know what's going to happen then they started calling several people at a time they went and the rest stayed…

> they unloaded us in the prison yard with dim lighting and of course it made us feel a little uneasy…

I didn't even know where akrescina was my first impression was it's hell. I was prepared that they would beat me I just sort of accepted it and that's it…

Tuesday, 8 September

I was turning my head and scanning the space, especially when I heard sounds behind my back. This is psychological self-regulation: figuring out where I am. Not to fall into a state where anxiety paralyses me. The prison guard shouts at me: "Face the wall, don't turn round!" I then turn back calmly to the wall and feel that I must resist. I chose for myself during those nine days not to look directly at the wall but to turn my head and look at the people nearby and to keep my hands down along my body, not to cross them behind my back, until I might be punished for it. A few minutes later, the guard tells me that in the army he was never called anything nicer than 'shit-face,' but he himself wouldn't insult anyone unless someone insults him first.

I turn my face to the wall calmly, taking my time to obey the command, and I'm proud of this tiny act of resistance as if it were a great internal victory. Intuitively, because my tired brain is almost asleep.

My last lover used this tactic in life: do something without asking permission and apologise if someone holds you accountable for it. I've always been jealous that he can do that, but it turns out that any knowledge, even the one you've only gained by watching, can come in handy one day.

I remember a guy I had white-red-white nails   which he noticed   and I got frightened   because he asked me why they aren't green   and I felt so uneasy   because I heard horrible stories about such things…   actually my mood as they were driving us there was fine   the girls and I   made friends at the police department   so on the way to akrescina we were joking laughing and   the cops who were riding with us   were also smiling etc then we arrive enter   our mood hasn't changed   then one of the girls said something   another one starts laughing   and this dude in a balaklava started yelling at us   like what the fuck are you laughing at   don't you know where you are   face to the wall   now and at that moment it was tense   because you felt their power   and you knew that it was absolute   and that they wouldn't ever be punished for anything   so yes then it got scary…

Quick inspection. Jacket, pockets, pants, shoes. Sign a document. Return to the corridor.

Tuesday, 8 September

they started checking us I think there was a policeman and a policewoman   they were surprised and asked I remember that   we were so young or something like that and so when   they put us on the record   they took me   for an inspection and we were alone with the woman we went in and she   body searched me groped everything and asked   what year are you in? I say in the fourth year studying customs administration she looked sympathetic I don't remember her words but I was also surprised that this person   understands the absurdity of the situation but still continues to do it and   I remember yes she felt sorry for me like   I shouldn't have done it because I'll probably be in trouble at the uni   because of this…

there was no fear   and I was rather looking at those corridors   the shabby corridors I think you also said that they are   very cinematic…

> Inspection. Two of us are ushered into a small room. Undress completely. I ask, "Completely?" "Yes." — "Even panties?" — "Squat down. Heels. The other one. Don't sleep!" Enjoying her power over us. "You'll come back, you'll like it here, I promise."

Tuesday, 8 September

complete undressing and squatting   but back then the head of the shift   was kind only later I understood what the secret was   so he said well lads be nice to us and we'll be nice to you   they gave out bedding mattresses no problem sleep   and in general they were sickly sweet ...

there was a man without a balaklava who said   if you behave well the trial will be today   and if you behave badly   you'll be here for three days. they   checked us gave us bags   and   took us to the first floor. it was frightening because   there were other   akrescina orderlies walking around in masks and balaklavas...

we   lined up along the wall were whispering amongst each other   and then   the four girls were taken to a separate cell...

we were all tired   the four   of us were taken to a five-bunk cell. everything was as you imagined   and probably by that moment I'd comprehended and accepted what was happening in a way...

107

Tuesday, 8 September

immediately at the entrance we were given bags from the volunteers with the most necessary hygiene items and we were placed in a cell in which one girl was already sleeping she knew how things worked there and explained them to us so we felt safer…

then they measured our temperatures dabbed alcohol on our hands but they didn't search us in detail we didn't undress maybe just our pockets were checked they said if we had any food we could take it with us and they took everything else and gave us some personal care things sanitary pads etc. there was a dude who said his name was kolya he wasn't wearing a uniform and another fat dude in uniform his fly was unzipped and I said like dude your fly is unzipped he started to zip it up and he said oh these IT people they see everything I said so why IT people? that's all they bring so in short this kolya led the way and I just walked next to him and he started telling me how everything was arranged there like don't be a troublemaker let's not get on each other's nerves the trial should be in the next three days I'll take you to the girls' cell they have everything there…

I asked the guard to move ▇▇▇ into our cell we could sleep on the same bunk but he was like maybe it's okay for you but we don't need these perversions. of course I was very upset…

Tuesday, 8 September

he took me to the third floor where there were already girls from the same march and there was a girl detained earlier she had some food and I'm walking and I realise that a lot of time has passed and I'm pretty hungry so the girl fed me well to be honest I didn't have the energy or wish for any kind of reflection or to even be shocked at where I ended up I brushed my teeth and went to sleep...

There are eight of us in the cell.

We don't fall asleep right away, first we looked around, made our beds and had a little chat. I expected the blanket to smell like sweat at best, maybe urine, and that there might be blood or something like that on it from the tortures which happened here in August, but all I find is someone else's hair. I thank myself for wearing a hoodie, because the hood is like a cocoon where I can hide.

I could smell it before I could see it the stink is actually the worst thing there. there are several floors in akrescina and they differ in level of comfort. there is a third floor which is comfortable and the second floor which is very uncomfortable it stank there were crumbs all over cobwebs cockroaches the toilet didn't work but I immediately thought about those people who were forty people in one cell because well there's very little space I don't understand how so many people fit there...

Tuesday, 8 September

it was very cold   so it was hard to fall asleep   but I managed to sleep a bit   I didn't fall asleep right away but I managed and by the way in the beginning well I felt quite alright but as soon as I lay down   I realised   the seriousness of the situation like where I am   who I am   what I did   I remembered everything   because I stay alone with myself   and I think I even cried a little because the stress somehow poured out of me not that I felt desperate it was just the emotions that I'd experienced   over the past few hours...

to be honest I was prepared for much worse conditions really I thought I'd sleep without a mattress fine okay   I'd already got used to the idea that everything would be bad so   when I came and saw that there were mattresses I was very surprised. it was cold but   we slept in jackets I didn't take off anything except maybe shoes...

Tuesday, 8 September

it was very cold   and we were afraid to use bedding   we thought it had to be full of fleas   or something even scarier   so we didn't cover ourselves with the warm blanket   we covered ourselves with some of our own coats   my sister and I slept on the same bunk we just hugged each other and I remember that the night was definitely very   long because   somehow you keep waking up   you wake up   and you see a prison cell   but still it doesn't feel real...

I remember that we   fell asleep with the thought of tomorrow's trial and that we had an hour left to sleep   would we be able to sleep...

it's been a very long day...

Like all your friends,
I hope they are treating you ok and will let you go soon. Worried about you.

Wednesday
9 September

They wake us up at six in the morning. Not all the girls have woken up yet, so I can go to the toilet without worrying...

I felt so   strange   to go to that toilet and in front of everyone I felt so   well   not so much   ashamed since this is a normal thing it's just that there are a lot of people around and the toilet is in the cell   it's good that at least it was had a door that's good   but otherwise yes   I was embarrassed...

They bring us two loaves of bread — white and brown — cut into eight parts. You don't want to eat them because they are very stale. Also, I feel a little squeamish because I don't know where the bread is from, whether it was at least cut with clean hands, and how many weeks old it is.

Afterwards, they bring us sticky oatmeal in water and very sweet tea... I try to eat, but I quickly give up. You can warm your hands against the cup: the aluminium cup gives off heat easily.

Wednesday, 9 September

I remember the food oatmeal it was horrible I ate two spoons of it didn't finish it and in the end I ate some bread and tea   I was grateful for that bread and tea I don't know   I rarely eat bread   but that time it was very tasty   and   I drank tea   it was very very sweet...

I remember that in the morning   they didn't wake us up at six as usual at akrescina   the bread was brought a little later   at seven or   closer to eight. I just remember that they didn't wake us up   they brought us breakfast   porridge   and tea I ate because   I realised that   well first of all I was hungry because   on the day of my detention I only ate breakfast in the morning   and   I actually didn't feel hungry because of all the stress but in the morning I did so I ate...

when they woke us up I experienced it for the first time   when you don't understand what time it is   in prison everyone has that   you don't know what time it is you can't even imagine what time of day it is because it was still dark when they woke us up they brought us breakfast   and in such an easy-going manner   something like   girlies here's your breakfast   it was oatmeal   with bread but   they didn't give us spoons and we were half asleep   so we just ate the oatmeal   with bread   well we tore the bread and ate   and after we'd finished that oatmeal they brought us tea I think and that man   the guard says oh girl so I didn't give you a spoon   and we didn't even think of asking because it seemed to us that we were in prison and if they didn't give us spoons well that's how it is...

Wednesday, 9 September

> I woke up because they started bringing breakfast to the cells and that guy greeted us so very politely and even kindly girls good morning here's tea for you and so on...

I climb onto the wooden bedside chest and from there onto the upper bunk, diving under the itchy navy blanket. Without taking off my jacket, I pull the hood over my head.

> I remember a man looked in and said something like girls don't worry we'll do everything quickly we'll judge you quickly. well I ate and went back to sleep...

> I woke up at six in the morning because I felt worried and wanted to read the updates but they wrote that no one was released and I knew that I needed to go to the court...

> I went to bed but couldn't sleep because of the nerves so I woke up around eight o'clock and I didn't know what to do next...

Wednesday, 9 September

I had a long sleep after that of course and I woke up from a scratching sound on my bedroom door I have four children they couldn't wait for me to wake up so they finally scratched their way in and rushed to me all together looking at me as if I was a hero to them they looked at me with admiration of course it was the most pleasant moment in the entire experience. my youngest son has asperger's syndrome it's mild autism he is closed off on himself he almost doesn't understand other people's emotions you want to hug him and you see how unpleasant it is for him so when my children came to my bedroom in the morning hleb took my hand and with tears in his eyes said mum I was so worried about you… and we hugged…

a beautiful, dry, sunny day of this strange autumn. I'm sitting in the kitchen, drinking tea and thinking about the porridge they'll give you there. is there a bed or not? a pillow? a blanket? the most important thing is that they don't beat you. everyone repeats this mantra. how quickly our value system has changed.

I'm the first of the eight of us taken out of the cell: "Out with your things." All my things are a pack of paper tissues and a pack of wet wipes, a bottle of water and an issue of Modern Poetry in Translation. I also grab the bedding — I'll be sitting outside the room where my trial will take place with it…

In the corridor, the girls have to stand facing the wall. The boys stand facing the opposite wall. I see a colleague of mine. Meeting someone I know here is exciting, you can have a word, but I worry: if we're both here, then who's doing our work out there…

I didn't manage to do anything although there was tons of work and at the same time you are there we are all stressed out   of course there was pressure from all sides both that you were detained and behind bars and that you weren't at work and the tasks had to be redistributed. we just couldn't cope with the flood of requests and messages in different languages while our skills were not enough to respond promptly   and deal with another part of the work...

I was one of the first tried.

we were ready to jump in the car   and pick you up if anything...

Naturally, I hope for a fine, but deep inside I know that I'll receive an administrative arrest.

when we were lying down   with nothing to do   a lot of thoughts came to my mind   and   to be honest   as strange as it may sound I could think about the entire situation   I thought that no matter what we have to move forward take some steps both for all belarusians and for myself   that time gave me a lot of thoughts so there was a plus to it...

Wednesday, 9 September

we found a mop in the cell a bright pink one unscrewed it and pushed the stick out the window and started banging on the bars the people who had gathered there saw us and waved to us then it turned out that one of the girls in the cell had a white-red-white flag hidden under her t-shirt she said let's push it out and wave it we started thinking that we'd better not because then they would start stripping everyone and searching them and they would come to us…

I sat silently I didn't say anything for or against it their arguments were like come on the flag in akrescina we'll be like djs of change it's a symbol the flag from the window of akrescina isn't it awesome and the rest said look you smuggled the flag they didn't even search you and you didn't even have to undress if you hang it now then all the other detainees will definitely be made to squat and the conditions will be much worse. but you see the conditions worsened anyway so if we'd hung out that flag well they might have worsened two days earlier what I'm trying to say is you can't play by their rules. but no one wanted to take on such a responsibility either like do it and then in short it's a moral dilemma…

and then again we were sleeping back then they didn't chase you for sleeping during the day and so we were sleeping you wake up from time to time and don't understand at all where you are and you go back to sleep. then they started calling us to the trials…

I was calling the secretariat of the ▮▮▮▮▮ court for a long time and pestering them I wanted to know if they were trying komar hanna and if so when and some woman kept redirecting me to her boss and I got through to the boss and they told me they don't know anything we either didn't receive the files yet or just received them we don't know at what time and like sorry. then ▮▮▮ and I went to the court and we also started pestering everyone there. finally we made it to the boss she said you know I can't tell you right away but write me a list and I'll mark those who will be tried with a tick so we copied all the names from some chat quickly and gave it to her she ticked the names and said all these will be tried here today…

I had to go first that's why it was scary because like you don't know what the workflow is here how it should happen also it's via skype and you can't hear a damn thing and it's so absurd that the trial is via skype and they still put you behind bars. like here's a laptop here's me and the bars I'm like what the fuck? there was a stupid question I didn't even hear it but now I know they asked me like do you trust the court and I didn't even hear the question I look at the cop next to me he's like say yes but I didn't even understand what I agreed to…

Like everyone else, I'm being tried via Skype.

A separate kind of torture is to sit there waiting: the employees who work in the offices along this corridor press the buttons that trigger a feeling of helplessness in me. I try to maintain my dignity and not give in to provocation. "Girls, you should come here more often, you brighten up our routine…" "Well, tell me honestly, why do you speak Belarusian, is it to show off or by the voice of your heart?" "Why do you say narmalna, is that correct Belarusian?"

Wednesday, 9 September

he started   pressuring you   by asking you questions first where you work   then he started   how did he say   something derogatory in horrible Belarusian something like zmahary   and when you started to counter beautifully all those   questions well you know he   is throwing some kind of tautology at you   and you reply beautifully in Belarusian   I was thinking damn hanna what a beacon you are   you're like a beam of light   in these stupid heads…

there was   an interesting man who I don't know exactly who he is maybe he was   the head of akrescina   of the temporary detention centre   specifically   I remember his face   dark eyes and light hair he's short and a little stocky   we kind of even   tried to talk about something and   have a discussion   but   the next time I was detained he drove all the girls hysterical in court   right during the trials myself included. but the first time he was   quite nice   and allowed us to sit on   the bench…

since I have a degree in history   I was there leading discussions about the white-red-white flag coat of arms pahonia   and   by the way one security guard in akrescina was arguing with me for a long time   and by the end of the day when we were already leaving after the trial   well I was telling them that they were beating people up there he said no   well so we argued about different topics and already at the end of the day he said even gesticulated to me before we left   we didn't beat we didn't beat it's the riot police riot police riot police and he gesticulated it so emotionally   of course they'll shift the blame   but here's what I thought gosh I only talked to him for a few hours   I don't work for the kgb   but how much information can you essentially get from a person   effortlessly…

I'm getting more and more fired up until they threaten me with more days of arrest. They could probably do it... So, they already know my verdict. They whisper with each other: "...that's not too bad..." Everything has been decided.

Wednesday, 9 September

by the way the policemen who argued with me in the corridor   sometimes their most weighty argument is now you'll get another report. and we could discuss and bring in arguments and then this and constantly you will get another report...

it was so absurd that it   dulled the sense of seriousness of the whole situation a little that's why I held on   to it. we spoke with him   very carefully in a half-joking tone   I think we started discussing the police torture he was like   well no as if we just follow orders we say but orders   can also be criminal and you are responsible   he says but we have no other choice   otherwise you'll   shoot and kill us all. we say no   that's not true   look at us we will not kill you   we do not wish you any harm at all and   it's not too late   to choose the good side. every time the situation reached a dead end or when we touched on something personal he'd immediately act like a boss he was like   that's it keep quiet or   you'll be standing   instead of sitting we were like okay fine. we asked him about his children   aren't you worried that your children   if all this doesn't end now they'll have to see   this horror too he's like   no my children won't be roaming the streets   so these kind of   stupid answers but   it was all   with humour because clearly he isn't stupid he's a smart guy he   knows a lot and   he also bears some kind of responsibility   I could see that he's   not from the lower ranks   if he could talk to us like that   but at the same time the mood was   as if we were flirting with each other we're girls and he   we're laughing it off but   trying to talk about some serious things. well that was   nothing really offended him   he somehow joked it off   as for us we're sitting outside the court room   we're facing risks   who knows what will happen at the trial   and how he can influence it...

121

Wednesday, 9 September

I was convinced that they would give us administrative arrest I had not a single doubt about it   because they had already started to detain people more actively   and I thought that although they were not detaining women one day they would detain women en masse as a demonstration. and I had a feeling that it would happen symbolically on the 8th of september...

Through the eye of the webcam, the judge is talking to the wall behind me. I'm not requesting a lawyer to be called (I don't have one anyway), I want them to give me a fine as soon as possible and I'll go home.

I talked to a lawyer and he said that if you didn't have children or this kind of thing you'd be jailed...

I'm repeating my version stubbornly:

I felt threatened by the people in uniforms, I felt terrified, we all felt terrified there.

well and she asks me what and how it happened and just a bit earlier with the girls we were discussing whether to admit guilt or not   and I said that I actually was going on a date   and then the police encircled   us I said that   I don't admit guilt   for going on a date...

during the trial my stance was I wasn't going to pretend that I'm a poor unfortunate sheep as they called us   I spoke quite confidently and I'd even say I challenged them   so it was clear I wasn't broken   I was defending my legal right...

Wednesday, 9 September

Nine days of arrest... I'm requesting a lawyer, post factum. The Judge Laykovskaya looks at me in surprise, "But I asked you earlier. You can write an application for appeal, ask for the form in the corridor."

I exit the room, sobbing.

after the trial   you came out sad   and started to cry your sensitivity   and sincerity touched me   it was as if you were   the beacon   in the system in which we find ourselves I felt sorry for you to be honest   in a fatherly way   I wanted to comfort you as a human being...

I was prepared for any fine   and they tell me   thirteen days of arrest I was so shocked   because I was absolutely not prepared for that   and I went through the stages denial anger those passed very quickly   I'm like no no this is impossible then I start crying then I'm like fine okay   and all that within just two minutes. I remember   there was one chair and the other girls were standing   I come out of the cage   and   the cop sees that   well that I'm in shock   I turn around and I don't believe that all this is happening   and he is like let her sit still a moment I'm like I'm already going to be sitting here for 13 days...

no one told us anything   no lists   well we kept waiting   and asking about the lists they told us they'll be ready soon   but they weren't   well the board showed only the timing of the hearings for administrative cases   under article 23.34. we waited waited and waited there was no information...

when he started to scold you   like why do you go to these protests what do you need there   why do you go what more do you need   and then the boss came out from the room on the right   and said that we should all be jailed   then he started to tell you   that no matter how long you protest nothing will change   and you started to cry even more I say everything has already changed   everything has already happened   and I say trust me   before the new year   and it happened in our souls   before the new year everything had happened if it hadn't happened   if huge numbers of belarusians hadn't come out   then how would we live if the elections had taken place   amidst all this   brutality? so many pustules   of this whole system have burst as a result. and then another policeman came up and said he checked where you work   so what more do you need   and he started to teach you reason   and you speak in belarusian so beautifully   honestly when you speak in this language   well it flows   it feels so   right it's as if you and I were sitting in the centre of europe and razmaŭlajem beautifully...

The man who was detained with us, also in a white hoodie, is comforting me and says that thanks to people like us, we will succeed. His sanity restores my resoluteness. He says that his wife is going to bring him a care package and asks what I need. Pen, paper and sanitary pads.

Wednesday, 9 September

Nine days of arrest. It's a lot. I hope you'll write great vieršy during this time.

I initially prepared myself for the worst for maybe twenty days of arrest   but when I found out it was nine I was actually kind of happy…

we were called into a small room   one by one   and   when I entered the room   the door was left open there were no police officers there were bars   a desk a laptop   and a chair I sat down at the desk   there was a woman on the screen   a nice looking woman   and she began to read from her document to me   so fast that I had no time to follow her as if she just wanted to get rid of all this once and for all as if she didn't see anyone didn't hear anything   so   she read it out   and asked if I needed a lawyer   then   if I had any objections   and finally she told me that I was fined   fifteen basic units. I was expecting arrest   and was very surprised when she told me   about the fine   and I don't even know what I felt more   relief or   I just   had some strange feelings then   I mean   I probably got so used to the thought   I wasn't upset no   I just   don't know how to describe it   I just expected the worst although usually I'm a very positive person and don't assume the worst   but   for some reason that time probably to make it easier for me I calmed down and   said that   I can endure this if it   will help our country   later   this is the price for our freedom and I   can endure this   it sounds pretentious but here it is…

my family hoped that   I wouldn't be   jailed   and so they stood near   the ▇▇▇▇▇▇▇ police department   and waited for me to come out after   the trial…

Wednesday, 9 September

of course I drew their attention to the fact that both the person who detained me and the alleged witness a policeman acted as a witness their testimonies were carbon copies of each other well I tried at least to say that I didn't resist at all I didn't sit down on the ground I didn't grab the policeman's sleeve but obviously no one was interested in this and as I found out in the end it doesn't matter whether you resisted or not everyone got their nine days of arrest...

They bring people from other cells, I see ▮▮▮▮▮. I ask the guard if I can approach my friend, he says no, and I say to myself: it's absurd to ask his permission, and I take off running to ▮▮▮▮▮, I manage to hold her hand for a couple of seconds and tell her my verdict. They also bring ▮▮▮▮▮▮▮, my other friend, and we rush to hug. Everything happens very quickly, and I, along with another girl, are being taken to the cell.

they gathered us from
a number of cells and
took us downstairs where
I met you and you said
that you'd been sentenced
to nine days. fuck me
I weighed up my chances
but mostly I still was
far from understanding
fucking anything where
I was and what I was...

Wednesday, 9 September

Before entering the cell we have to leave our shoes outside and put on black rubber slippers with the cell number on them. The other girl's name is █████, she is also sentenced to nine days. We try to sleep. Hours of waiting. Feels like we were put into a tin of condensed milk and from time to time we are dripped onto a spoon from the pierced hole. I know that we should be transferred to the Centre for Isolation of Offenders. All of the unknown makes my anxiety grow.

the hardest thing by the way is   waiting   you sit and wait the trials take a long time   and next to us the men from osvod were tried so we chatted with them and we were like   you are real men thank you   at that time the policemen were passing by and we stress that   you are real men   not the police…

I gave them   my bag with   hygiene items because well because I received a fine and the rescue guys weren't given anything   no toothbrushes…

I haven't brushed my teeth since the morning of 8 September and I dream of at least a toothbrush, but for now I have a finger and water. I need to tie my hair. A wad of toilet paper in the cell is tied with a thin rubber band cut from a medical glove, I take it off and fix my hair in a ponytail.

Wednesday, 9 September

what was that trial like? a weird crackling skype   I didn't hear a damn thing   my witnesses didn't show up   that mangy old goat read something from a piece of paper   are you mad   what resistance I weigh fifty kilograms. I say I   don't agree but please give me a fine   she's like okay   thirty basic units...

they took me to the exit   to release me   and in their   slobbery ledger they couldn't find my last name   and the date when they brought me there   I say well yesterday or already today   and that cop had a short circuit like yesterday today how is it possible   then eventually they found me and released me   I called ▓▓▓▓ brother   he rushed to pick us up. the ninth of september   was such a warm sunny day   we brought our car   back from kamaroŭka market where we left it   and we went for a bath of course. I had bruises on my body as if someone had been kicking me...

I had several bruises too apparently from the moment when they pulled my legs and arms but I didn't feel any pain in the moment...

Wednesday, 9 September

in the end we only got to the next hearing we thought that was the beginning but in fact it was not the beginning at all   we listened to three girls   as they were tried   the judge   actually looked very sane but still gave everyone   fines   and found them guilty   and it was so strange she says no need to stand up sit sit yes of course make yourself comfortable   etc.   and then she gave those   stupid   fines and found people guilty it was just   a very big dissonance. at some point ▮▮▮▮ was released   but she'd got to see you   she wrote to us that you were sentenced to nine days. when did they even try you?...

                    purely by chance   you met a friend of yours in the corridor in akrescina and told her   and because she got a fine she went out and told all of us   about you   IT country what can I say   that's how people learn the news. I found this girl   and asked her about the details she said that she was upset   she didn't expect you to be   sentenced for so long or sentenced at all   but you are alive safe and sound and that was the most important thing at that time...

do you plead guilty   under such and such article? no I was walking behind the column   didn't offer resistance and he was like for this five and for this four days that's nine days of arrest. I was so indignant and he packed his stuff and left I was sitting next to the screen disconcerted. as I found out later   on that day that judge gave everyone nine days...

                    it didn't matter if you had a lawyer or not   they gave the maximum fine   thirty basic units to girls and fifty to boys   it was the same for everyone   well I was also sure that you would have a fine. they gave fines and it didn't matter   that you had evidence that you weren't at the protest   some people were just walking home because they lived there   they brought their passports with registration address   to prove they really were just walking home...

What to do?

My only option is to lie down, try to sleep. Another sister in crime is brought to our cell, we introduce ourselves and chat but we can't get rid of the tension. For lunch, they bring us dodgy boršč and cutlets made of fish bones. I can't eat this...

Wednesday, 9 September

that fish cutlet fuck me if it was made of fish it was made of bread mixed with fish bones and skin...

I remember that I couldn't eat there at all the only thing I tried eating there was boršč it tasted like vinegar with salt and coloured red but it was the first food I ate there...

At least we have an opportunity to establish contact with the warden, and he brings us a bag from volunteers: a toothbrush, toothpaste, sanitary pads, paper tissues. I talk him into bringing me paper and a pen. "Only if you return the pen, 'cause all my colleagues always take my pens and don't give them back..." I want to write everything down, but all I can do is stare at the blank sheet of paper.

he just brought us food and then probably he sat down next to our cell or he offered us a second helping or something like that and ▇▇▇ asked him do you have a smoke? he then called her over and quietly gave her some cigarettes we asked him what time it was then we heard voices in the corridor what's going on there tell us we asked him he told us that people were sitting there waiting for trial then we asked if there were a lot of people so he was kind of our eyes...

there was one employee who well he clearly wasn't a good person but he helped us. I didn't know that you could take some things from your backpack with you but I had my period and there were tampons in my backpack so I told him that I have my period can you get me a tampon from my bag and he was like so why didn't you take it with you but he went down to the ground floor found it and brought it to me...

it was already one o'clock in the afternoon I think or two o'clock in the end we left that fucked court and   I started calling their secretariat again   I was asking them where you would serve your arrest. everyone was tired and said we don't have such information. so we decided that we had to prepare a care package urgently and we started to put it together urgently   I think we even finished putting it together urgently back then you could still bring care packages every day and it was a blessing...

I went home to our shared flat and started to collect important things quickly. I wanted to put something nice that you like but I didn't know what you like so I started looking for something that I myself would appreciate getting and well you start to consider how much so that you can wash them so that there are clothes to change into. in some way it's an interesting experience you know preparing a care package for someone and you wonder what would be good for them to get and I had some warm clothes like that purple fleece thing I thought maybe they wouldn't give you blankets at night and it would be cold the fleece would help... I met a boy who volunteered there while I was standing in line and he was like we have to repack it all because they won't accept it in this form so we started sorting everything in small bags...

> I remember very well that feeling when I was in the store grabbing those transparent plastic bags to pack the things for the care package everything needs to be packed in a separate transparent bag I was unrolling them straight from the roll and stuffing them into my pocket I felt like a criminal...

the time they accepted care packages in the centre for isolation of offenders was from 10 am to 12 pm and in the temporary detention facility from 2 pm to 4 pm we missed those slots but someone told us that if a person had just come from the trial the first parcel could be brought from 6 to 8 in the evening the volunteers somehow managed to arrange it we needed to come in person to sign up for the queue for a care package we signed you up. we arrived at akrescina maybe by 7 pm I found your flatmate with a bag handed her socks they listed it all and then we had to wait. the procedure was that a volunteer who goes inside at some point has a list they probably talk with one of the workers to check according to the lists whether a person is there or not we came to the volunteer can you clarify if hanna komar is there and he says hanna komar isn't here. what shall we do? she's either in the temporary detention centre or she was transferred to žodzina. we went and rang the doorbell of the temporary detention centre and you weren't there so in žodzina? it was wednesday and in žodzina the day for care packages was only wednesday so we thought we didn't make it. upset we think oh well hanna will have to wear the same clothes until next wednesday but shoot what was she even wearing? we're like damn what was she even wearing? we really hoped that you at least wore trousers and had a jacket so you wouldn't freeze there...

Wednesday, 9 September

at first I wanted to write you letters every day   but wrote only one and realised that damn   I fucked it up   at the same time I posted things on twitter well because I had no one to share them with   I always posted photos from the rallies on twitter   and some time before your detention you texted me in our telegram chat babes I'll clear my history to be on the safe side   so I wrote in a tweet just yesterday she cleared her history to be on the safe side and today she was detained I hate the current government and everyone who is involved in this lawlessness...

when I found out that ▆▆▆ and ▆▆▆ were released and you were jailed   well to be honest I was fucking shocked   because I couldn't get my head around it   and I became very worried about you because   I know that you can probably endure anything but you know it was just   this fear   that I think we all experienced after the first nights on the ninth of august that something horrible could happen   in jail...

134

when I got out I felt lost at first for some reason I thought that no one had come for me at first I didn't see anyone I didn't see my mother I didn't know what to do but I saw people who were helping volunteers they immediately came up to me and there were also people who were waiting for other detainees they started asking me about the detainees   did you see such and such a girl there I try to answer trying to remember if I saw her I was still in some kind of shock that I got out   and from the amount of light that I saw out there   but still I   was holding up and when I saw my mother   I burst into tears   even though before that I was holding on with all my might and   stayed calm...

we went out and were handed our care packages when I saw the packages I thought that our friends were prepared for us to be jailed for several years   because my sister and I had four bags each and they were full of sausages sweets and stuff. we asked the policemen to please take one of the bags for our friend he has a trial   they took it reluctantly   and you know we're exiting the prison gate with these bags like some old ladies   and by the way you don't think about someone waiting for you there you can only think about your friend who stayed about the others who've been jailed and how lucky you are to be released but your conscience is bothering you. some people are in a bad way   but you are well again   and somehow it feels unfair...

I knew that I would get a fine but still I was happy   I put my signature went down   tied my shoelaces and took my belongings   well it's still somehow   it's a really happy memory   how we go down the stairs   go out of the gate   there are people standing and waiting for someone   well my dad was at the trial actually in the court so he was driving to akrescina but I was passing on to the crowd   the names that I could remember. at that time there was still a camp   outside akrescina   so I went there   took I think a coffee   drank it   talked with the volunteers   found ▆▆▆▆   we exchanged contacts that's all   then my dad arrived   well we took someone else to give them a lift   and I remember that we were driving   I saw that they sentenced you to nine days   and together with my dad   we started thinking how to send you a care package. I even by the way   then tried to   find your relatives   and find you on social networks   and I found your page on vkontakte   and found some distant relative of yours   some cousin   I don't know   I wrote to him   that this and that you were detained and might need a care package   but it can only be brought by relatives   he answered that like we are very distant relatives we don't communicate at all and don't know each other. I was like well okay   sorry then…

our friends   relatives   colleagues   were there to meet me and I look at how many people there are and they are there for us saying something smiling   and I am in some kind of   shock   I think there's no need we were taken and we were released we didn't deserve any kind of I don't know a minute of glory   nothing big happened but we were greeted like real heroes…

and then   we were driving in the car   and my dad was telling me something   there was a lot of media coverage of that march   and since the photo of my arrest of the moment they led me to the police van together with my sister that photo and video got on the internet and the following morning my dad received a call from my high school   which I finished two years ago   they offered to raise money   asked how to help   maybe something else is needed   even one of the deputy head teachers with who I had a good relationship   called and so I was riding and thinking wow that's awesome…

Wednesday, 9 September

in the beginning it was okay we had fun we were making jokes about all those terrible things then the trial then it was sad because we had to spend a while in jail and then it was just routine the relentless routine of prison...

I didn't know where ▓▓ my boyfriend was but for some reason I thought he was in the cell next to ours and we were all tapping through the walls žy-vie-bie-ła-ruś I was tapping on my side of the wall too but I didn't know if he was there and then the girls who had a trial at the same time as him told me he was in the cell next to mine and they said ▓▓ received fifteen days of arrest and I hear the boys being brought into the cell next to ours so I start tapping loudly on the wall and someone from there starts tapping just as loudly and I realised it was ▓▓ then we are sitting and talking with the girls when I hear his voice through the ventilation and it turned out that we had taken the same bunks and it was so nice to talk to him. he said he was upset that they sentenced me to so many days but that I was great and I could handle everything it really cheered me up at that moment...

We got upset about your long sentence. The day flushed down the drain. In the evening we went out for a beer and bumped into a big column of people with white-red-white flags! In Čyžoŭka! Beautiful, cheerful people.

137

Wednesday, 9 September

My pen is taken away. In the evening, we are transferred to the Centre for Isolation of Offenders. ▇▇▇▇ and I are placed in one cell, and ▇▇▇▇ in another one somewhere.

I received two care packages   when we were being transferred to the cio   they lined us up   along the wall   I was standing there   not expecting anything   at all because they said that only relatives could bring care packages   and then   my last name is called   the officer's like   what's your sister's name? I say ▇▇▇▇ but she can't be here   he asks my patronymic I say ▇▇▇▇ but maybe   he's like let's go quickly because it was already late. later I was told it was from volunteers   they told the police I was   an orphan from ▇▇▇▇ and I needed that care package   then I'm standing again my last name what's my husband's name? I was stunned what's his name so I peeked into the list ▇▇▇▇. well it was nice to receive them but   also   there were men who didn't receive any care packages so   I poked around my bags   there was a guy standing next to me I took something out and I said here take this...

> I'm not expecting a care package, convinced that out there, everyone just goes on with their lives. When they gave me some basic hygiene products, I calmed down. I'm morally preparing to spend nine days in my white hoodie, imagining how it will look and how I'll be stinking when I travel back home by public transport...

that feeling that the world outside of this does not exist I can relate. of course I was happy with everything that I received in the care packages especially comfortable clothes but most of all I wanted to receive some kind of message but there was none...

I found a phone number on a bottle of water and then on a chocolate bar there was a slip of paper that said ▮▮▮ we are with you and a little heart signed ▮▮▮.

I burst into tears...

when you were detained I posted about it on facebook and many people from our mutual friends abroad responded and wrote to me there were also a lot of comments under those posts a lot of people wrote to me in private and asked and my posts were shared...

Are you safe for now? Is there anything we can do, for you? Or to help Hanna? Also, if what you need is rest, you should rest, not answer my questions. Take care! You are brave!

Wednesday, 9 September

Thank you for writing updates and for the work you are doing. You shouldn't have to live in such a way, where you have to search for your friends like this ♥

Heroes!! It sucks that you have to handle this situation, but thank you for everything that you do ♥♥♥

Thank you so much for the updates and for all you do ♥ You are amazing! I have the deepest respect for you and all the other brave belarusian people who are peacefully fighting right now. And so very sorry for what you have to go through. All my love and best wishes

we created a   chat   and were running around with care packages we distributed who bought what. now it's remembered with a kind of optimism   because so many terrible things happened   after that   now I can see how much support there was back then and so many people around   half of these people have either left or   are in jail now   but back then   it was frightening   I had a big shock   because we'd been in touch a lot back then   there weren't so many people detained and you were the first of my close people who was detained plus you're a girl it was worrying...

In the corridor, where we are waiting to be transferred to the CIO, facing the wall, the man who had comforted me after the trial saw me, he says that his wife didn't bring a pen, but he puts a pack of suški into my hand. It warms my heart.

my wife always feels what is needed   she found out what was needed   and immediately organised some hygiene items   for everyone who was detained   together with the women volunteers she gave someone a lift right away and then basically everything was ready for the care package…

In this place you want to stick with those people you've made friends with, and every time they take me out of the cell, I get tense because I don't know if they will separate us or keep us together, who the new people will be and whether I'll be able to get along with them.

you depend on the others there   in general we were like-minded people   the only issue was that the guards have their own kind of scheme   they constantly mixed the detained among the cells   we were moved   to the second floor   it looked like that cell had been painted   recently and the light was dreadful and my head began to explode I even woke up at night from a headache   I was even dousing myself with cold water and things like that…

first they put us in a cell where   the toilet didn't work I went in right away and checked that the valve was working   so the toilet would flush   we protested and said move us to a different cell we won't go to this one there were twelve of us so   they took us out searched us again   and transferred us to another cell…

A cell for four.

One of the girls is an activist, and I'm amazed at the paradox of the world: first you go out to support the detained activists, and then you end up in the same cell with them. The second girl is not political, she received five days for trying to steal a bottle of vodka from a store.

I shared the cell with a girl she was maybe thirty-two and she almost went on a bet she had some money but you know just for kicks when she was drunk she said I'll nick some vodka and that's the story. she was alright everything was fine but there wasn't much connection between us because she was out of the context and when they brought you two I was so happy I thought finally some politicals so I could find out the news you started telling me that people came out for kalesnikava and what was going on in general. before you a woman was put with us for the night she was in all the photos when you'd just come out at the kamaroŭka and the first arrests began she is a former athlete so cheerful and upbeat she told us stories and cheered us up and she saw how that other girl had not a clue what was going on then we had trials on the second day the girl was given five days and I was given ten and she spent half the day ranting that she stole something and they gave her five days and I didn't do anything wrong and they gave me ten so that woman told her look what a country you live in maybe you'll finally think about it etc. then you two arrived and it cheered me up...

███████ and I are given two sets of linen, but one mattress to share... To our questions, the female guard replies that she doesn't know where the other one is, it was there before. She promises to think about it in the morning, but for now, it is what it is.
I unload my treasures on the table: napkins, toothpaste, water, a book, suški.

I remember that I hadn't eaten or drunk anything for two days by then   so the girl and the woman were giving me their tea from breakfast because my blood pressure had dropped from dehydration. honestly   I'm sitting and thinking that I need at least three spoons of this disgusting soup to comfort my stomach   I'm bringing this stuff to my mouth   and everything inside me is churning I realise that I don't know how long I can hold out I really wanted to eat but   I couldn't. what we got from the tap there could hardly be called water. I remember that you came with a pack of suški   and with water   and I looked at it like it was some kind of incredible treasure honestly, I'll never forget it I actually ate two suški and it felt so good   that I finally ate   then I saw your book and I hadn't received care packages all that time for two days in total but really two days without a care package was hard   I saw that book I thought my god civilisation is returning I was as happy as a pig in muck...

> It's very cold in the cell because the window doesn't close, but it's better than no oxygen and the smell of the toilet. Two of the girls take the bottom bunks, and we are 'settled' for the night on the top bunk. We hug each other to somehow fit onto it together, but I keep rolling to the edge all night, because I'm worried to move too close to this girl I barely know, even though she seems to be completely unfazed by the situation.

I thought you two were buddies   who got into trouble you know and that's why you are like well alright. at night I was attacked by cockroaches so   I jumped up to the upper bunk because I couldn't sleep I was seeing them everywhere even with my eyes closed. I remember that I was deciding I either sleep with cockroaches or in the cold okay I'll sleep in the cold I slept in a hoodie right next to the window...

Wednesday, 9 September

Maybe it's for the better that the light is on at night too, otherwise it would be rather creepy...

I was looking at them   at those guards   for example there was a boy he was well   young and he was   good-natured   he always wanted to talk with us about things   he'd lean into the feeder how are you doing there are you alright   and at night when no one else was around   he was alone in the corridor   he would talk with us for a long time even when we wanted to sleep he still wanted to talk with us   well   about life   we ask him how did he become like this he says well I couldn't get any other job I'm an orphan no one wanted to hire me I tried everything   and I had to live somehow I lived with my grandmother   his grandmother raised him   and he says the last place I tried was prison   and they gave me a job in ████████ and so he kind of   grabbed onto this chance   that's how his fate turned out. well I tried to understand I say you were here   on the ninth tenth and eleventh of august you worked here and saw everything. and he said you don't know anything nothing happened he denied everything and he said that on the contrary he brought people water and bread   what a good man. I say well how can you stay here   and it was interesting to watch that he was so nice with us he could bring us more tea etc. but when someone else came   for example someone above him in terms of rank he immediately looked down to the floor   and   didn't even look at us didn't say a word he immediately   fell into   a slump...

Stay strong, and I hope this will be over soon! I'm proud to know you! Big hug.

Thursday
10 September

Thursday, 10 September

It's humiliating to stand facing the wall while the female warden is inspecting you roughly as if you were a sack of potatoes rather than a woman too.

no one really came into our cell   well probably in the morning and in the evening there was some kind of inspection and they turned over our mattresses   but the rest of the time   we did what we wanted   that is we slept…

The toilet stinks, so when we find a fragrant soap in the care package, we put it in the middle of the table, as an improvised air freshener.

▬ is telling us her story, because last night we had no energy to talk.

I arrived to akrescina at about twelve o'clock at night there were two other guys with me who were drinking beer on the street some time after the rally on sunday and they had some protesters' gear with them. I was escorted by a young guy I can say he was nice well as nice as it was possible he was sympathising with me the whole ride well I was also angry they deceived me five minutes ago I think to myself what use is your sympathy to me keep it for yourself you work for this system anyway. I'm riding I'm cold he's like why are you wearing only a t-shirt I say well because they took all my things and promised to let me go home he says I'll try to get you your hoodie we arrive at akrescina and there's this crazy man I had an ring in my nose and another girl had some kind of industrial piercing bar in her ear and she couldn't unscrew it just like I couldn't get my nose ring out well he started yelling I got frightened for the first time probably some kind of fear of physical threat appeared because he started yelling that I'll bring pliers now we'll rip it out I don't care about blood I just need you to go into the cell without these earrings or he says you'll sit outside in a puddle without food or water and fight with each other's earrings until you get them out you won't go into the cell. well I lost my shit I was a bit frightened but I couldn't keep quiet and told him that what century are we living in how are you talking to people why are you threatening us do you hear yourself? he said I'm not discussing it with you either take out all this crap or it will turn out as I said. I somehow miraculously got the nose ring out and they brought small manicure scissors for the girl she's standing and with shaking hands she's unscrewing this earring blood is coming from her ear I stand there in shock trying to help her I can't do anything either in the end she got it out and at about two in the morning we ended up in the cell. that young guy actually got me my hoodie he went somewhere and quickly while they were bringing me to the cell shoved the hoodie at me and said stay strong I'm like okay thank you…

We're looking for a way to cover the window with a towel.

We play word games and laugh at silly jokes. Laughter is saving us, it distracts us and soaks up the anxiety, my body relaxes, 'fight or flight' mode turns off for a while. I read a bit of poetry in English from the Modern Poetry in Translation, look for beautiful lines and, translating as I go, I read them out to the girls.

"Perhaps you yourself are the red lights of the lighthouse...".

They brought us another mattress, now I have my own space, where I try to sleep, curled up. All this is monitored by CCTV over the entrance.

the camera is right here above my head and I could physically hear it clicking and the red light coming on seemed like it turned on several times a day for a couple of minutes that's the feeling I had...

Rasolnik for lunch. Its smell makes me sick, I flush it down the toilet, although the drain can get clogged. The girls say that we'd better wash the dishes with soap after we've eaten, because they may be washed just once a day, and the rest of the time they circulate between us.

Thursday, 10 September

we had a delicious rasolnik there on one of the days after I was released I realised what the trick was. I think in the same days one infamous presenter of one state-owned tv channel filmed a story about wonderful conditions in akrescina and their delicious boršč. I saw that rasolnik in that tv episode I remember how we were surprised like damn such a delicious rasolnik but it was a one-off thing of course…

of everything I ate with pleasure in the cio let's say it was bread and compote well or tea everything else was horrendous those sausages those fish cutlets and even their oats were so terribly overcooked it was impossible to eat…

After dinner again, "Out with your things!" And again no one explains anything to us, you can only guess that they are taking you to the prison in Žodzina. We're kinda relieved, because we heard that the conditions are better there.

when we came to the red church the following day we were greeted and applauded sincerely girls you've returned I then realised a formula for myself that often after detention people come to treat the protests differently some are afraid to go out but I noted for myself that if you go out immediately after being released you serve your sentence and return to the streets then you aren't afraid...

I'm not giving up; I'm trying to write an application to obtain my case materials. "Give me a pen," I ask the man who is taking us somewhere. "I only have one pen," he replies. They are all like that here: you ask for something, and they use the opportunity to humiliate you even more. "Yeah-yeah." "Maybe." "Ask there," to all your requests.

a couple of times we asked them for a pen to write an appeal against the court decision but you can be sure no one gave us a pen...

suddenly the three of us were called out of the cell and I was like alright only politicals something's coming. then they lined us up in the corridor and divided us into two groups we were all standing there in the corridor with our noses to the walls and then I got my first care package I was standing there and shouting my name with my face to the wall. she was like what and I shouted a care package a cleaning lady was mopping the floors there she checked and said yes there is a care package calm down we'll give it to you and that's it they gave us the packages there were about twenty-six girls and the rest were boys...

Thursday, 10 September

Myself and the girl that I shared a bunk with are taken to another cell. It's warm there and the girls treat us with sweets. We find mutual friends who are also somewhere around, and we are kind of getting used to the new place, when we're both removed from this cell and brought to the exercise yard and left there. We meet the other women, including ███████, who we waited in the cell with after the trial. Finally, we can all exchange news to understand what's going on. We guess that we are being transferred to Žodzina, but our questions remain unanswered.

Four women are taken away, and we stay there for another hour and a half. It's cold. We sing.

we were loaded into the police van I was riding in a so-called glass for one but there were two of us in it and we each had a bag but I dug into mine and found a book it was harry potter in belarusian translation and inside there was a postcard how they let it through I have no idea I open it and there it is covered in writing by my friends and family and I'm reading this postcard in the glass in the police van and such strange emotions laughter and tears but very timely of course very timely it was to find that postcard in a police van couldn't have been better...

they brought us to this chicken shed we stood there for about six hours it was cold and it was drizzling your singing was cheering us up then we arranged for a guy to bring us some cigarettes he brought us cigarettes then they took some of the people away and we were probably waiting for the last police van I guess...

We want to go to the toilet, but no one comes to take us anywhere, and they don't respond to our banging on the iron door. I sit down and pee in the drain, hiding from the CCTV. To keep warm, we're jumping and dancing. My feet are freezing in sneakers, and someone suggests that I should put sanitary pads instead of the insoles.

when we were about to be sent to žodzina and   the boss of the shift or whoever he was said   like well lads   no one beat you right they didn't beat you up they didn't abuse you   none of those scary things like we hear about ourselves so I'm even scared to come to work. I felt like spitting in his face because before that we were standing   in the exercise yard   and we know what was done   in these yards that were used instead of cells and on one of the walls   the word fuckers was scribbled in congealed blood. and in that very yard   there is a hole with grating   and there was shit on it obviously people   went to the toilet there   if they took you for a walk for an hour you don't go to the toilet in the exercise yard...

Finally, we bang our way inside, into a cell, to warm up. The cell is right in front of the entrance, and we can hear something happening in the corridor. We whisper with the boys (who've just been brought in) through the slot in the feeder, to see if we might know any of them, and it's just nice to have some contact. You take hold of every smallest contact, it reminds us that we are not alone here, and it could also be a way to get some news.

> then we had to find a person with the same patronymic as yours and we couldn't I posted on instagram but unfortunately the girl with the same patronymic agreed and then backed out because her mother is a police officer so the girl doesn't participate in such things...

the lists are coming from the cio oh komar hanna is still there. we mobilised found a henadzieŭna special thanks to her. so i'm in a taxi and tell the driver where I'm heading he's like what happened to you i'm like well my friend was detained i'm bringing a care package he's like oh I see I see so we arrive and I ask how much to pay he's like oh nothing you know you have this happening no need to pay. it was so sweet...

> the previous day we signed you up on the volunteers' list and we double checked that you were there. all good we handed them your care package there were no issues at least from our side it was sent and then on the lists the following day I think you were marked as already in žodzina. we are like well our package may have been wasted because from what we knew they transported people to žodzina at lunchtime and we brought it at lunch. so we were angry because we didn't know if you received it or not...

I was sitting and thinking fuck what's going to happen to her there how can we help. I was added to the chat where everyone was worried about you they were putting together a care package googling how to do it better and talking I thought how awesome that there's such great support...

Thursday, 10 September

Finally, we are taken out into the corridor, and near the wall we are waiting for transportation. They start handing out care packages. I'm still convinced that everyone out there is just living their lives, and yet I'm holding my breath, so much I want to hear my name. And I hear it! I run through the corridor, take it and burst into tears. I'm not alone. They didn't forget about me. I'm not alone. There are people out there. I'm standing with my face to this stupid wall and sobbing with happiness.

it was so comforting before being transported to žodzina ▮▮▮ was standing by the wall I passed by and touched his hand. I really needed it at that moment some kind of physical supportive contact…

On the way to the police van, we hear that there are people behind the wall. They are chanting something. "Long live Belarus!" or something like that, and it makes us happy, and full of emotion, we crawl into the glass — four of us into a tight, dark glass.

"Girls, looks like my period is about to start, and I'm not prepared."

"Well, do what you need, it's dark here."

I do what I need to do: pull down my trousers, attach the sanitary pad to panties and pull my trousers back up. I feel no shame. In fact, I feel grateful to the girls that they neither had any questions nor were disgusted. My period started just as we were being transported, and with an interval of about twelve hours, the other two of us, four cellmates, had theirs too.

Thursday, 10 September

In Žodzina, we, terrible criminals, are met by the military with dogs. In case we turn nasty. They lead us into a room with walls covered in white tiles. I remind myself that I'm a poet, which means I can find poetry in everything. Since it's boring to stare at the wall all the time, I'm studying the tiles. The tiles seem so thin and frail, they need the wall more than the wall needs them, so they are huddling against this wall, huddling so hard that thick folds of sand (the kind swallows make their nests from) protrude between the tiles. It's intense. We are told to stand tighter together so that everyone can fit. One of the menacing soldiers has his mobile phone ringing, the ringtone is a song in Russian: "Quietness, I so want quietness / I want quietness in the broken silence / I will fly freely with a light wind..." As if vomiting, my laughter is rolling up, and although only a short laugh reaches my throat, I feel a relief, because we all feel like laughing, everyone I can see when I turn my head around without being noticed and shouted at.

firstly shock   the dogs...

yes I got terrified I was the first to get out of the police van   and   there was that light in my face and the dogs were barking I got frightened...

yes those old tiles when they put us   along the wall like this   and   that anteroom I don't know what to call it this strange place where there's not much space anyway but they tell us to move tighter together and make space and they keep bringing more and more people in and you can see there's not enough space for you...

Catacombs, long and full of anxiety...

so they brought us to žodzina   the reception was horrible dogs all around and a shitload of guards standing around with their truncheons   so we went through their catacombs I went first for some reason he kept turning to me and yelling faster faster he walked in front of me and was hitting the wall with a truncheon non-stop some guys there got hit for turning their heads...

those military men   were aggressive   a guy in glasses   a tall one   damn clearly he doesn't get laid so he shows his aggression   because he feels his power over the lads   yes clearly he was bullied at school and now he's taking revenge when they were walking he threatened them something like you'll be going squatting he shouted like keep your distance   when we were being led down that corridor. I thought they were leading us to death because   well   they can't lead you to a good place   down such a corridor   because you're walking   this crazy corridor   these shoes without shoelaces   they flop   and I see a guy walking in the very front   poor thing it was so hard for him in those shoes   and also he was limping. and the panic what will happen with you where they're taking you   you're walking   this rope   some kind of wiring or what   it's endless   horrible   like a dungeon   and this dim light   and you're trying to see and remember at least something so in case you escape   you understand where   some clues   so that later if needed you could tell where you were and what you saw...

Thursday, 10 September

We're standing in the corridor, facing the wall, the four of us. The boys have been taken somewhere, and we are waiting for inspection. Two young officers keep watch over us: one is tall, and the other is short.

The chief officer asks them if they would like to inspect us themselves and immediately adds that they shouldn't because we, the women, might like it. Why are these prison guards looking at us and discussing something? "What, are you choosing one of them for yourself?" and they laugh loudly.

We don't find it funny. I'm figuring out how to behave in order to preserve myself. Be more careful, not as daring as on the night of the detention…

Don't smile at them, don't look attractive.

They are flirting with our youngest one, she's only nineteen. Everyone here seems to consider it their duty to ask us why we go to rallies and if we get paid. This stupidity makes me feel helpless, and I want to bang my head against the wall.

I definitely decided that I wouldn't try to be friendly with them   I realised that   I'd be okay sitting in a cell but any interaction with them   was stressful   so I'd rather not to talk to them   not respond and generally   keep it all to a minimum and   not to smile not to giggle I wouldn't allow myself to do that   for me   it would really be self-betrayal…

> It's late, probably closer to midnight, and we don't feel like answering their stupid questions at all. But they won't get off our backs, they want to know where we work — and how much people in IT are paid. They discuss the dormitory where they live when they work their shifts, and they discuss their families. "Dad calls me Uładzik…" I could have been their teacher at school ten years ago…

in žodzina the conditions were tougher   I just   looked down for something a cop came up to me   and hit me with a truncheon   and a doctor who was with us he spoke in belarusian too   he was very emotional   so they beat him up   we were standing along the wall   he felt unwell   and dropped out of the line   they were like where the fuck are you going! and they started hitting him with a truncheon   I say he is unwell so they hit me with a truncheon too   well   they were so cruel   their major   grey-haired   shift supervisor   was the most aggressive he didn't like my eyes and didn't like my bald head and he told me like you knew where you were going you were prepared you fucker…

I knew that we had to be inspected   and   all the waiting   when will they inspect you   and clearly you'll have to undress   and this one will now   inspect. you understand that they took you to fuck knows where the guys were taken somewhere   it's only us four girls   and you can't do anything   I was waiting I just wanted it to be over and they would take us to the cell…

Thursday, 10 September

I'm leaving for an inspection.

A very sane woman in military uniform. She has beautiful rings on her fingers. She doesn't make me undress completely, only down to my underwear. I tell her that she is very sane, unexpectedly. She replies that she actually serves in the military and has nothing to do with this prison, she was just asked to do an inspection of the women.

I was inspected   by a nice woman   we had   a good conversation she asked me about fifteen times   like don't be afraid if you were beaten tell me I say no they didn't beat me and then I take off my trousers she says are you sure you weren't beaten I wonder why she's so concerned I look down at my thighs and see they are all bruised   well   because those mattresses in akrescina aren't mattresses at all of course the metal bars left quite an imprint on my body...

flowers I had dried flowers with me they were taken away she said that they will die I say they won't die they survived akrescina   and the detention before that...

I've returned from the inspection, the girls are telling me that this boss scratched our youngest girl's back...

And he continues mocking us.
"Well, you'll have a discotheque on Friday."

My God, what is a "discotheque"?...

I think there were two bosses and they were both bipolar I have a lot of questions about this system in general who they appoint to such positions   they are really scary people they are   partially insane you can expect anything from them one moment he is standing there joking then in a second his eyes change and he starts yelling...

While we are standing facing the wall, in an office next door the boss is yelling at the detainee because he didn't put his hands behind his back. He's yelling and threatening that the detainee will follow their rules whether he wants to or not. The two young guards are flirting with our youngest one. ▓▓▓ starts to cry. ▓▓▓ tells us to pull ourselves together, in a firm voice. I reach out to pat ▓▓▓ on her shoulder. "Take your hand off her," Uładzik commands.

I say girls calm down   don't show your weakness don't show it to them   on the contrary it turns them on even more... but he started saying something like come on don't cry no one gets beaten here he offered some water... and before that they'd been yelling at the guys it was frightening they're real psychopaths now they're normal but in a second they can kill a person...

Thursday, 10 September

They want to separate us into different cells, and I ask them in a gentle voice to let us stay together. Finally, we are in the cell, together. Such a relief.

well when I got into the cell of course it was funny   very funny   but like I was in a sanatoryj   a really big cell for eight people   I met some people I know well   there and of course it became much easier. the girls all had care packages too because it was care packages day the day before and of course I hadn't eaten for almost three days at that moment of course   I almost went crazy with joy   you can eat and you can drink normal water   and you can wash your face normally too   and   there are even blankets...

once in the cell   we all first introduced ourselves 100% people with higher education...

Thursday, 10 September

We are given a bit of time to settle in, we have time to clean up a little and wipe all the surfaces with wet wipes. Then the bright day light is turned off. In the care package, I find things that'll be comfortable and warm to sleep in. I put on two pairs of socks, sports pants on top of my leggings, a sweater over a T-shirt, and another sweater on top. We're hitting the bunks...

you don't know what will happen   when the morning comes what will happen...

Stay strong!!! We will win:)
We're worried for you:(

Hanna, we're with you
♡ ♥ ♡ Love and hugs.

Friday
11 September

Friday, 11 September

There is a slit in our window frame, and it's freezing cold and hard to sleep. You can sleep in pairs, but on these mattresses it's difficult even for one person to lie down without hurting your bones. Only in the foetal position my bones don't ache... But I can't lie like that all the time: my body doesn't rest. I notice that my arm hurts. It must have been pulled when I fell as I was being arrested. I did notice the pain earlier, but have become aware of it only now.

Wake up at 6 am. The schedule prescribes that the mattresses must be rolled up and we're not permitted to sit on the bunks until 10 pm. To be on the safe side, we roll our mattresses, but no one checks them, and we don't do that anymore. There, in general, you'd rather not try to follow their rules too hard, so they don't feel like complete masters. Don't follow the rules for as long as you can.

the daily routine is like this in the morning you have to roll up the bed linen we've rolled it up we sit   and we sit we wait not clear what we're waiting for   and they open the feeder they check you   for them it's a kind of entertainment or what was it...

Chocolate is saving my breakfast. Although afterwards, the porridge was often salty, then nuts came in handy.

Friday, 11 September

the first porridge that was given to me I ate it with great pleasure   I even thought that I would cook it at home if I could find the recipe. just ordinary oatmeal in milk but for some reason it tasted so good   like home-made...

We are given one mug of tea between two of us. ▬ wishes for them to have one wife between the two of them. We're laughing!

in general   the girls were quite cheerful   I'd even say it might have been a kind of defensive reaction   well because clearly you aren't gonna cry for the thirteen days that they jailed you you need to somehow   colour your life   humour is a very good tool   irony and just some   sarcastic   jokes jokes about these guards about all their ongoing stupid trials...

You can warm your hands holding the mug. There's only a cold water tap in the cell. I'm morally preparing to wash my hair in seven days.

I was also posting all sorts of updates about you and tagged your page and your ex wrote to me like thank you so much for writing about hanna and I was like damn dude I'm in a comatose state fucking hell I can't accept gratitude I want to just burn and kill I was also supporting your sister. my nerves were starting to give up answering everyone and it was quite difficult to coordinate in the end we united in a chat and it was just wonderful…

it was complete hell it was probably the hardest time for me over the past six months well because when I go to the protest I have only myself to worry about but we didn't know how you were or what you were and all that messing with the care packages it's also nerves and emotions and stress and all that and I'm basically not quite a sociable person and it's always difficult for me like I don't know to get involved in help of that kind my initial response is always a stupor but at that moment I realised that I had to somehow get out of my shell well because I couldn't manage on my own so I created a little chat and when I did I laughed because I called it literally well I couldn't come up with a name for it so called it I couldn't think of a name…

for me personally it was much easier to be jailed than to wait for other people to be released afterwards…

Friday, 11 September

Above the sink, a small mirror with a crack is squeezed into the wall. I see myself in the mirror for the first time over three days. Not that I was worried about my looks, I saw that the girls looked alright and assumed that, therefore, I did too. I just tried not to touch my hair.

To see yourself in the mirror means to single yourself out in space. A child goes through the mirror stage between six and eighteen months, identifying herself or himself separately from other objects for the first time: this is I. We can't see our own faces directly, just as we can't see some parts of our body. In prison, my body exists separately from consciousness. The mirror is my only way to make sure I'm still me. But it's not a girl looking at me,

it's a woman, tired and aged.

we had a mirror   for the first time in   four or five days   we could finally see ourselves in a mirror   I saw that my hair line was uneven   and started to beautify myself   so immediately you feel like a human being and it felt so nice   here I was   my dear self all good   all in its place...

I saw myself in the mirror   black circles under my eyes it was probably from dehydration and because there was no fresh air...

168

I've received a little notebook in my care package!

Friday, 11 September

> I wanted to send you
> something really nice
> something   beautiful
> I wanted to send you…

And envelopes, but I don't remember anyone's addresses except my parents'. What should I write? Do they know what's happened to me? I should probably comfort them. And yet pass the censorship.

I wrote to my parents that I'm in Žodzina, we are fed here and not beaten, and that I didn't do anything wrong, I was simply exercising my right to freedom of expression and freedom of peaceful assembly. It was important for me to write this, I wanted my family to know that my detention was unfair. I wanted to be strong. But I needed support…

your friend ▉▉▉ called me and said ▉▉▉ just don't worry but hanna was detained. of course I got awfully worried tears came to my eyes I thought gosh   what could such a young fragile little woman do to the police to have been detained. it was frightening when we didn't know where you were for a long time   we were looking for you   for a long time   and in the moment you don't know what to do I called ▉▉▉ often we talked she comforted me all the time she said don't worry   don't worry. I was particularly worried   the most important thing was that they wouldn't use physical force against you because it's horrifying   especially knowing from hearsay what happens when girls and men are detained   well it's horrifying I was really concerned about that. I was worrying a lot   for a long time until we found out where you were and what happened to you…

Friday, 11 September

I found out from your sister. well how can a mother react   of course I was   very much upset   I was very worried about you. I cried. I could barely sleep. I was thinking about how to help you what's the point of going to Minsk we didn't know where you were   no one told us in the beginning. I was worried that   they would abuse you   and conditions there are terrible   I was worried about your health   I heard that they beat people there and that there weren't any facilities   to wash yourself things like that. and I couldn't bring you a care package where to bring it how I didn't know. of course I wasn't ashamed   and just recently I met a teacher who worked in your kindergarten she remembers you well   she asks how is hanna I say my hanna's life is in full swing   she goes to rallies and she was even detained once the teacher says what a great girl do you support her? you have to support her she says. and her husband is a former policeman I ask her and how he reacted to all this   she says he doesn't even want to hear about lukashenka...

> how I reacted   I agree absolutely   with our authorities   that's how I reacted. I thought you   got in serious trouble. because I knew   in principle   your mood for this kind of situation   so it was predictable. knowing your attitude   to this system   I knew that you were there and you weren't innocent. you were with those   who were   guilty   and you were for them   entirely and completely...

my relatives are a separate topic they spent all the three days before my trial by akrescina   we saw them from the window   and we shooed them like go away   go   you don't need to be here but they   would come as if to work   and sit there   some brought blankets or foldable camp chairs   it was still warm then. while I was in jail   they organised like a flash mob   they made posters   in support of me   they went out to the rallies with those posters   and put them in the places where I like to be   one of my friends   who played football scored a goal and lifted his sports t-shirt   and there was another one underneath and it had a print saying freedom to mauliuda   my friends' children would bring their little posters too   my brother and his girlfriend also arranged a support action   and   also my colleagues   went out on the balcony   with posters. my boss himself   stood under akrescina prison for three days together with my relatives...

After an endless number of attempts, I handed my letter over to an officer, the one we called a "fat pig." "You didn't have to stick it down like that," he tells me, opening the envelope effortlessly. Later I found out that my letter never arrived.

Friday, 11 September

Dear Hanna!

I sent you my first letter yesterday. But I sent it to Akrescina. Today I found out that you were transferred to Žodzina. Some sergeant perhaps will read that letter and throw it away.

I often look at some troubles in life as just a short span of time. That is, any trouble will end one day. So I tell myself that this will end too. I used to not be able to apply the same approach to the situation in the country; now I can. We just have to do what we can and wait. You radiate optimism every time we meet. I hope that mine will reach you now. And that nothing can upset you. You can't see it, but I / we love you, we read your poems, there've been your photos and your lines all over Facebook…

I was going to   come and somehow try to send you a letter   on monday or I don't know   to come to pick you up   we didn't know yet that you'd be transferred   it was all very   strange back then and   kind of new. on friday evening I returned to minsk and to be honest for me again because it was some kind of super odd   unfamiliar experience   I didn't realise that I could at least try to write you a letter   or   maybe send you a telegram   I mean something like that   at least…

they wrote me letters   but I didn't get any   still it was nice   I didn't know they were so concerned…

171

Friday, 11 September

Toilet. Without a door. I feel ashamed of using it. You keep in mind that you'll have to every time you eat.

well yes   you had to learn to excuse me shit in front of everyone   so you learned what options did you have…

▬▬▬ received a newspaper with arrowwords. I haven't solved them for maybe ten years, but doing it collectively is quite fun.

I honestly have no idea how it happened but   somehow we slept for about sixteen hours a day. we slept at night then you think god there's nothing to do okay let's lie down again and everyone's asleep again…

Later, we used that newspaper as an engineering tool to regulate the window: closed when it was cold and opened when we needed some oxygen.

Being in a confined space shared by four is the kind of circumstance where you become close quite quickly. So here we are chatting about the most intimate things: our loves and exes, how things did or didn't work out, about sex.

Friday, 11 September

those conversations we had in the cell it's also interesting how much stuff came out maybe in ordinary life you hid it somewhere deep afraid to admit some things to yourself but there somehow you just suddenly shared it and began to treat the situation somehow a little differently a little psychoanalysis behind bars...

Why are we here?

I wanted to do some sports and for some reason I was craving for buckwheat and so they gave me buckwheat on the first day at akrescina. the girls wanted to stop reading social networks and I also wanted to get enough sleep because outside we worked from morning till night and there was no time to get enough sleep. some wanted to stop reading the news and take a break from it others wanted to start reading books. stasia literally a few days before her arrest complained to her husband that she had no new female friends that she was all alone here you go. so really everyone wanted something like that and everyone got it...

the protests had been going on for over a month   so my psychological state was I don't know   critical I constantly had I don't know panic attacks I couldn't concentrate on work at all   constantly going to the streets   the stress was just enormous all the news that you read all the time   so in this regard probably in some sense   I don't know I either waited or well I was even glad that   they had taken me   at least I saw what was there because constantly just reading about it and   not knowing what awaits you   let's say on the other side   well it was getting tiring. so   those nine days were   I don't know like a breath of air right to take a break from   the news and from browsing through it constantly   a very unusual kind of   holiday...

With these half-jokes, we try to explain what makes no sense: why some of us received administrative arrest and others fines, why some were sentenced to 9 days, and others to 11, 12, 13... In fact, it's a lottery. Sooner or later, we would be detained anyway, because we had been to the same 'walks', standing next to each other, yet strangers. On 8 September, the circle just closed.

██████ washes her hair under icy-cold water and leaves her black hairs in the sink. She draws eyebrows with a graphite pencil. She sleeps.

thank god she slept a lot because honestly   her rare moments of wakefulness were hard for me... she's completely ignorant and not intelligent to me ████ isn't the revolution's face   because the revolution is so   intelligent   kind   and smart and ████ I think she got herself into this by accident because of her youth excess rather than   for say   the idea. the lack of an independent opinion of her own point of view   she simply fell into the general wave or something...

▰▰▰▰ **keeps lists: a list of activities for the day, a list of what to google when she gets free, a list of what needs to be put in a care package.**

Friday, 11 September

we made a list of things you wouldn't think of right away. I received the best care packages in terms of functionality   because everything was there   even things I wouldn't have thought of   I was like how do you know is one of you imprisoned too? they sent me star balm   I wouldn't have guessed   and they sent me a blanket too   not everyone got a blanket in their care package   but it was great to have. I love blankets   and it was great   because those blankets that we had there weren't that nice they were actually horrible   so if you had your own blanket that was just amazing…

▰▰▰▰ **crosses out the days in an improvised calendar every night. You try not to count the days, because if you fixate on your sentence length, it seems endless, and it's hard to hold up. But still, you do count the days.**

I knew that I had no right to get angry because you can go crazy but of course it was like a red thread in the background   awareness that some   not particularly bright people were simply taking away my most precious time   and absolutely unlawfully. but I tried to shift the focus because I knew there was little point in that…

Friday, 11 September

now it seems that nine days is ok not much but back then   nine days it seemed just   well   I was tempestuous   I remember that in the beginning it was kinda ok for me because we were busy with the stuff you know like   preparing a care package   then the trial transfers we met with people or were in touch   or met new people   and then you naturally get worse   I got overwhelmed on thursday or friday I cried a lot   well you know for all the reasons   because tiredness had been accumulating and I knew that I needed to force myself to rest at least a little not to collapse   plus I felt scared   it got scarier because we realised   that if   women are taken so we   will be taken next time. it was just you know some kind of blackout   when you were holding on and holding on   then things became really bad…

The last days of the warm autumn. They say it'll be slush and humid soon.

I feel like taking photos of everything here, so many details, as if it were a movie or an installation. If not physically, then at least emotionally turn filth into art. I remind myself that I am a poet and can paint with words. Write things down, write it down, write. I can't. I don't want to. Stupor. At the PT lessons at school I couldn't jump over a barrier, I sped up, ran, ran up to it and stood, petrified. My body doesn't want me to record this, doesn't want me to remember it, it wants to release me from here. Everything else is self-deception.

After dinner, the Russian song "I'm Free!" is played in the corridor. We don't know whether to laugh or cry. Then the 'disco' time came… Fortunately, there was nothing horrible about it. They turned on the radio and led us into the exercise yard. We look at the sky above the wire. It's sunny. We cheer up, ▬▬▬ and I dance to Russian pop music playing on the radio. I dance because I can. But when I see that we are being watched, I shut off and contract immediately. I won't give them the joy of seeing me dance. In the last few minutes, we just shuffle about.

so he took us out for a walk and closed the wired net and the door behind us and according to the rules you aren't allowed to look where they bring people in and out don't look under any circumstances. and ▇▇▇ she was confused she either didn't hear or was absent-minded but she stood near the door they were closing us in and she just looked at the boys who were being led down the corridor for a walk and he started yelling at her what the fuck are you looking at you're going to get the fuck out of here now and he even hit the door with this baton I think and I stood there and said are you mad or something that you're yelling at a person do we live here or something how the fuck are we supposed to know your rules...

those walks I wouldn't even call them walks in fact we would be taken to a cage for 10-15 minutes and you walk there back and forth or go around in a circle you only see the sky but of course it's at least some joy the sky I remember the sun came out we all huddled up in the corner under the sun basking. when nice music was playing we danced there was like a disco I wished we could have stayed even longer in such moments...

Friday, 11 September

In the evening, the smell of shashlik reaches us. It's Friday, maybe the employees are really grilling shashlik. It's disgusting and disturbing. I can't let go of anxiety because I remember what happened on the 9, 10 and 11 August, although we were 'comforted' at the entry that no one is beaten here and we'll be well fed. We were told several times that people were not beaten here. Were they trying to convince themselves?

it's friday and I thought that I need to sit quietly and not sing songs because they'll get drunk and who knows what will happen I thought that they might beat us up...

How sad that you don't see these last summer sunsets.

Thinking about you every day.

Saturday
12 September

I had a dream that no one was waiting for me and when I returned from jail, no one even noticed...

for nine days I went out of my mind with worry precisely because I didn't know where you were how you were and what was happening with you...

I was calling žodzina zealously   is hanna komar there? the man answered me yes you are the tenth person   to ask about her   she is here   I tell him don't worry another ten people will call   he probably at some point could simply pick up the phone and say yes   hanna komar is here any other questions?...

Menstruation is difficult here: lying on an iron bunk, going to the toilet which has no door, taking your time to brace up...

The girls in the cell next to ours loudly sing Hraj, and we tap against the wall "Žy-vie-Bie-ła-rus", the only way of communication with our kind, and it travels to the cells on either side as well and to the floors below and above. An answer from the cell next door, then the call spreads throughout the prison, and we calm down: there are a lot of us, we are together.

we tried recalling   some lyrics of the songs   that everyone knew   we recalled them and sang there was a guy with us who sang really well I don't know almost like an opera singer   we were listening to him with rapt attention...

For the second day, an untouched loaf of brown bread lies in the middle of the table. It's made right here in Žodzina by the inmates, maybe that's why it's better than the one we had in Akrescina. The food here is better in general, probably because the prisoners themselves cook, in fact, for themselves.

And still, we don't touch it, we have our care packages: biscuits, chocolates, marshmallows and nuts. But I feel uneasy that it's lying here. It's bread, it's food, someone probably needs it, and it hurts me a lot to understand how this is humiliating, that for someone this tasteless, low-quality, god knows in what conditions and by what hands baked, ugly prison bread is a joy, because they have nothing better.

we had our food   like sweets in one place and all the other food in another   we had different shelves for different things. we put everything together because   everyone was in the same situation anyway plus someone received two care packages or three   and others only one   so to somehow share   for everyone to feel comfortable we put everything together...

Saturday, 12 September

Today we handed out newspapers in Čyžoŭka and ate watermelon. I keep thinking that they must be feeding you some kind of crap there. Although a friend told me that the food is like in a school canteen. Well, at least there's that. I remember I even liked some of those dishes.

My hand is reaching for my hair, but I remember in time that I haven't washed it in a long while, and lower my hand. To our questions and requests about the shower, we hear, "How will you return the favour?" and "Maybe, if you behave yourselves."

I'm thinking about the new Constitution and that I'll need to study the project carefully so that we aren't deceived again.

so we are sitting and stuff   well we are in quite a good mood and somewhere around lunchtime   they bring in a   respectable-looking man   in a suit   with a beard and   a bible in his hands   we were joking that it must be the   educational activities on the schedule   we really immediately thought that they brought us a priest   who'll be preaching to us   and then we saw his trousers   one leg of his trousers was completely torn   at the seam   that is it turns out they took him as he was in a suit and shoes...

Saturday, 12 September

and we swept everything away the cell was really clean and tidy nothing on the table or the floor everything was shoved away hidden   we sat down I was like something's missing   forgive me I don't want to offend anyone's feelings but we had a small book the new testament I put the new testament on the table and was like now it's good   so when the inspection comes in it's crystal clear eight girls and the new testament. it was then they took our clock away...

A guard brought me my thyroid pills, but I ditched them. They should be taken an hour before breakfast, but how can I find out the time?

we were lucky that we had a clock we could at least see the time. there was this crazy screw   he snatched the clock out of my hands he kept running around looking for someone he really probably thought that we were going to make a bomb and blow him up   because every time he came to us his eyes were wild he was running around looking for something he thought that we were plotting a coup there...

Saturday, 12 September

Corridors are being mopped. They tell us that we'll have to mop out our cells too. Disgusting.

But it's disgusting to live in this filth too.

I was hoping that   the following week   we would see each other   and I don't know maybe I could somehow support you and do something   but then saturday came and   on saturday   I was detained at the women's march   and   I thought   already knowing that there we could be transferred that I could theoretically meet you   in žodzina   or   meet someone   who you'd been in the same cell with…

and then there was a women's march   for which I   was late. I messaged ▮▮▮▮ that I would join her and I was half an hour late that is by the time I arrived she'd been detained. of course I also got enough trouble we were escaping the police around the opera house   but then we still did our march   and this was the march that   took place despite the arrests…

Shower!!!
Warm shower!!!

Two of us under the same shower? Easy. Four people to use one men's deodorant? No problem. My friends sent me a men's deodorant, and the girls rushed to sniff it with joyful excitement: the smell of a man...

A nice young guard, we called him Partisan, is on duty on our floor today. At least we thought that he was a nice one...

we took a shower once during the whole time   and even then   they offered us their company   I understand that it'd stay at the level of jokes   obviously   because they just wanted to wag their tongues but still   the most unpleasant sensations when you hear all this   being in all this   I just felt that they were pressing me into the floor   with their energy of stupidity of some kind of bluntness in general   I just wanted them to leave as quickly as possible and not loom around let me serve my term don't show your faces just even...

we asked if we   could take a shower   and he asked if he could come with us   like if I can come with you then I'll take you   in that context. once the male guards   took us to the shower   and then we covered   the little window   with a towel...

Saturday, 12 September

> In the evening we're reading a book aloud. ▮▮▮▮ is reading, and ▮▮▮▮ and I are listening, lying or sitting on my bunk, covered with a blanket, or cuddling, or we just snuggle, shoulder to shoulder.

it helped when we read books together
it felt   more peaceful and then   physical contact   without it those   thirteen days would have been much harder for me…

I kept that book   chicken soup for the soul   my director sent it in the care package   there was also a note inside we're waiting for you   I recognised his handwriting…

it was nice to finally read   in everyday life there wasn't much time   always you're in a hurry going somewhere   and then   the moment presented itself to finally read   ▮▮▮▮ gave me an interesting book what was it called   the light   the unbearable lightness of being and it was set   just during the times of communism   when the soviets occupied   the czech republic and there were also like repressions persecutions   you know   also you couldn't write anything oppositional in the newspaper because they would immediately   come to you and could even fire you from work   or ask you to write in this newspaper that I   renounce my thoughts so you know   it's intertwined and no nothing has changed   over the years…

> I'm worried that I left important work tasks unfinished… I feel guilty.

an avalanche of news fell on us every day and each was more absurd and harsher than the other and we worked from nine to eleven...

Saturday, 12 September

I was very worried about my family my mother my sister and that was what weighed on me the most...

We talk a lot because when we stop, anxiety returns. When it comes to possible options for the development of events, I want to hide, curl up or not exist. But none of us doubts that we will win.

Saturday, 12 September

I could see that they would detain me because I already saw that I had nowhere to escape. we were standing with linked arms I was helping someone to climb over the terrace and they were able to escape. I chose not to resist and the only thing I got was a kind of hard grip let's say of my hand but in general they detained harshly they threw one girl into a police van and they were shoving a girl in and she fell to her knees and they kept pushing her in anyway but I don't remember everything because I collapsed in the police van. well I think it was okay simply because no one seemed to be afraid and someone was filming a video on instagram someone was calling their relatives someone was posting on facebook well I guess we didn't understand then that this was all kind of serious and maybe we thought that well like they would let us go or I don't know that they would hold us there for a few days and then let us go but after they'd transferred us from the police van to another one with cameras I mean it was dark in the first police van there was no light there for some time and then when they turned it on I remember there were inscriptions and in the ▮▮▮▮ district police department where they brought us they kept us outside in a garage or something and there was definitely blood and it was visible and identifiable and it was frightening because there were zip ties on the floor well in short it was a very I don't know some kind of a pressing feeling that you're standing and you know that there's almost a 100% probability that they beat and tortured people here…

In the evening we sing songs from my youth. Although we're of different ages, we all know these songs

Saturday, 12 September

singing
songs was
my favourite
activity...

the girls sang folk songs   alright   everyone sang the song mury and all that   but they sang folk songs and they all knew them from somewhere   and with multiple voices   it brought tears to my eyes when they sang like that   when it was late   and after lights out   they sang so quietly and so beautifully   well I just   consider myself lucky to have been around such people...

"Good night guys, good night ladies." Maybe people like him brought water to the detainees on 9, 10 and 11 August...

Saturday, 12 September

I need some personal space, but I get it only when the day light is turned off and the night light is turned on.

the first five or six days there was total hubbub noise   then people started getting out   hit the bricks so to say   plus everyone was tired. I still can't imagine how I stayed sane with so many people in the same space all the time with the toilet just three centimetres away from you...

I have a   niggle   I've a problem with sounds   I don't like other people's sounds   I don't like when people eat when they snap their fingers   and   I'm also shy with strangers I can't approach them and say what I need I used earplugs all the time for me food was a constant torture   and   it all accumulated accumulated and accumulated   but   there was no aggression among us it was super cool we spent so much time together   and kept everything   safely inside. and I felt support   although when I feel bad I try to close myself off...

you can't do anything   you   can't go   and free   anyone but you just wait until they let your friends out   and you can't talk to them can't ask how they are and how they are doing if they're okay   that kind of thing   I'd come to your room to feel   at least   a part of you   like the creams you used or something else you know   to feel a part of you   and in general   for the room not to be empty   when the light was on I found it easier   to feel some kind of presence...

The night light is on all night, I fold a T-shirt and put it over my eyes. This is what my ex-husband used to do: even though I gave him a sleeping mask, he'd still cover his face with a T-shirt to sleep. I hear the small slot in the door open, and someone's looking at us...

Saturday, 12 September

everyone complains about the moon that it somehow shines in one's eyes but for me it was fine because I covered my face with a hood when I needed to and if there'd been no light at all I would have felt very uncomfortable. even though I like darkness I didn't want it there in žodzina and at the same time this dim light you can write something down for yourself and the mood was I don't know romantic or something. well it was a nice time but it was better to fall asleep quickly to not to think about anything. it was easy to fall asleep the first couple of nights I had all sorts of bad dreams and then it was fine...

later when we figured out the daily and nightly routine what to expect we felt safer...

It's getting colder at night. I keep thinking that it's even colder in jail.

191

Sunday
13 September

Sunday, 13 September

I'll never forget this fucking freeze...

Nothing bad is happening, except for our freedom being taken away from us unlawfully...

I was concerned after all the situation is totally different when you are completely deprived of all freedoms and the prison guard decides whether you can go for a walk today or not whether you can go to the shower or whether you can't whether you can turn the light on or off all this is no longer in your power you just sit there waiting waiting for freedom it's hard especially psychologically physically I could take it okay I'll sit in a cell it happens that you sit at home for days but they just treat you like a terrible criminal as if you robbed someone beat them up but you just took to the street to defend your freedoms seriously? it's very insulting and humiliating that they treat you like some kind of trash even though you essentially didn't do anything wrong and that's what depressed me the most...

Sunday, 13 September

you know what   I wasn't worried that something bad would happen to you there I was somehow sure that you'll be fine   but for me the most outrageous thing is when my loved ones face injustice. for me this is particularly painful to know that a person is in jail how is it possible? it's awfully hurtful it's a personal hurt it's as if you yourself were hurt and you   don't know how to help you don't know how to fix this situation. it's not even an injustice   so absurd it is   it's so untrue   like   it shouldn't be like... there's not even a word for it I can't put it together it's so evil this is probably facing evil in its purest form   I just don't understand why we have to go through this...

I remember coming to the office and being like   can you imagine she's in jail   can you imagine she's jailed for nine days   eight days   seven   a week has already passed she's been in jail for a whole week do you understand we have been living for a whole week and she has been jailed...

I'm studying the cell: it seems to be completely made of metal, because both the wooden floor and the wooden table are the same milk candy colour as the metal frames. Here we are supposed to feel guilty and repent, but instead we are filled with a sense of the injustice of what is happening to us.

the repressive machine it had already been working right so I knew because others had been through it how it all happens that they feed you cabbage how everything there is like there is nothing to do just read books. so I knew basically that you weren't there on criminal charges but this is just a stupid repressive machine that jails you for ten days so that you reform yourself supposedly and learn to love your motherland properly so this is just a waste of time the last warm days were wasted I felt sorry that life could have been lived because it passes and even ten days are very important and you're jailed for nothing for nothing at all wasting your time for what reason do these miserable people have the right to take away this valuable time in your life and for you it's ten days and for others it's years why do these miserable people have the right to take away your life. this felt so unfair to me simply because summer was leaving autumn was coming and in this period of the last warmth you are sitting in this stuffy and miserable horrible cell and for what? and you also pay some money for this for the fact that they serve you there so to speak...

In captivity, all we talk about is how we'll judge them all by a fair trial.

Sunday, 13 September

I had a breakdown I just thought I didn't know what to expect   what would be happening   would I be alone would they bring someone would something terrible happen next   in short   I don't know I feel like all the potential catastrophic options went through my mind   and   to somehow   cope with the panic I wrote a diary or a letter to myself   about how I   hate this system for   what they do to us and that   I couldn't wait to finally have fair trials so that these people would all be punished. in the evening of the same day they transferred me to   the centre for isolation of offenders   and then the following day they transferred us from there to žodzina. and in žodzina they searched our packages   the huge bags that we arrived from akrescina with   and   one of the guards found this page of my letter   and took it away and I was afraid all the time that   something would happen to me   but since nothing happened I think that he just threw it away maybe he felt ashamed   I don't know...

Sunday. We're wondering if people will go on the march today. Wondering and hoping.

we kept a spoon   on sunday   and banged on the radiators with that spoon until they took it away from us. actually on sunday we had   a march in the cell   and we marched around the table on sunday we hung up   a poster   saying that fighting for one's rights is not a crime...

Sunday, 13 September

there was a march   on sunday   I was very scared to go   but realised that I simply had no choice like how could I not go   while you were in jail   because you did   and I would stay   at home and we came to the march   and it was a march through   puškinskaja   we went around the palac shopping centre to   the minsk arena and at some point   as we were walking in a big crowd from under the bridge behind puškinskaja about five police vans drove into us   and I was standing there thinking here we are   we'll meet with you there and then they stop   they see that there are a lot of us and they drive by   and we almost reached the minsk arena then we turned to walk back   and when we were marching back   the riot police squeezed us from both sides   probably three times   we ran through some kind of parking lot god knows how we managed and I remember I came home   and   sent you a video in the chat   that I'd been at the march   and even the sun came out to help me not feel so sad and somber...

"Will you take us for a walk today?"

"Maybe. Individually. Depends on how well you'll ask, hahaha…"

Sunday, 13 September

> we didn't go on a single walk twice we were about to we sat prepared in our jackets then something changed and in the end we didn't go anywhere we heard others walking we were told to get ready and in the end we still didn't go anywhere. that's why when I think on tuesday we actually hung a sheet of paper over the chow hole demanding for us to be let out the guard who was delivering food he liked the joke…

I want to listen to music with headphones… Frühling in Paris by Rammstein. I have a long list of the songs which I'll listen to when I'm out of here.

> I missed good music and coffee most of all I wrote to all my friends in letters when people were released they took the letters outside I wrote that please I don't need anything just bring coffee…

'When I'm out of here…'

is one of our most favourite topics, although the closer to the day of release, the more stressed out I feel, my nerves give up, I want it to come sooner, but time isn't going to speed up.

Sunday, 13 September

you're doing your own countdown plus you're trying to invigorate the people around you because often the conversations were like damn we still have a long time to spend here   and I used my favourite technique   I said look   the day after tomorrow liuda comes out   and the day after that you come out   and the day after you I come out   see so soon and so simple then everyone laughed and felt better immediately. of course in my head I was counting the days but I didn't tell anyone about it   because what's the point of saying it out loud you just drag a couple more people along with you no way no no no...

it's a particular experience when I come home and know that you aren't just away you are in jail   and it hits me every time   well loneliness first of all and   the understanding that you   are not very well right now and that you are actually in a state of   unfreedom...

"What time is it?" "Time for lunch."

like all of us I figured out the time by meals lights out and wake-up calls...

Sunday, 13 September

We've gathered all the plastic bags into one bag and played battleships.

of course they tried to have fun   we made checkers and chess from bread   in žodzina we also had bowling   we made bowls and a ball and rolled it   along the bench…

we were taught to play   prison poker   it's like you use   not cards but balls   you throw a ball   and two balls come out   and the dice show the poker combination   in the prison jargon   straight flush straight four   and the more points you get   the more you win…

I was making sketches   I sketched situations or jokes. there was an inspection once   and we had all sorts of knickers and socks   hanging on the window bar   so a guy came   our window didn't open   well the guy came like I'll open the window for you now won't I and he was some important guy and it was very funny to watch   that boss poking our knickers and socks with a stick. the guards who came afterwards told us off and told us there would be an inspection   and that inspection turned out to be that same guy   and it was very strange   because they yelled at us   and told us to put away those socks and knickers   and then the same guy came who had already poked them with a stick…

I was being creative I made a car from soap using my nails…

Sunday, 13 September

It's so interesting how we share everything here: food from the care packages; a cup of tea, one is drinking while the other is sipping from it with a spoon, because it's hot; bunks, you can sit or lie on any of them, with your legs folded and wrapped in a blanket.

you know I didn't see things as   mine   it was all shared. when we arrived   we were unpacking and maybe   on the second day we decided to sort things   so that everything had its own place   and somehow   we began to put everything in one place   because anyway we kept it all together on the table   the food and stuff   so our personal things   became shared. we also had common shelves   with   pens and paper   toilet rolls   and some   household supplies   well because again some received a care package others didn't   and you didn't want to be stingy in those conditions. we had a shelf purely for books everyone put out what they had because   some girls read very quickly and we exchanged books so it was easier to put everything in one place for some kind of order...

We introduced a punishment of twenty squats for every swear word... In the evening, my body is aching from squats.

I actually exercised because usually you couldn't make me do it but there   I did squats and push-ups because I had so much physical energy my muscles were yearning for it...

we started exercising right away   a set of push-ups fifty each   starting from one   then squats...

Sunday, 13 September

I'm waiting for the night light to be switched on so I can have some quiet time...

in our prison cell
the four of us
share everything:
liquid white
and sticky ochre light
bed squeaking
the cold curling up
the sun behind the thick window
fresh air from the gaps
between window frames
free trains rumbling
iron doors clashing
tapping against the wall
'long-live-be-la-rus'
warm water in the shower
deodorant
a newspaper with crossword puzzles
the voice reading aloud
thickened time
questions
curses
nightmares
and the very words
'when i'm out of here...'

media started writing about you publishing your poems it was very nice...

today is Sunday, it means, there'll be the Heroes March

really warm to see all these people, and yet, it hurts a lot to see how many people have been suffering on the journey to our freedom...

202

Monday
14 September

Monday, 14 September

our cell was midway along the corridor   practically every day they brought new people in and on sunday night especially. I remember how people were taken straight from minsk to žodzina because there was no more room so all night they were tossing people along the corridors   boys were examined and interrogated. they were asked if they had any injuries   and we were sitting and listening   there seemed to be a doctor although I'm not sure anyone got help. and that mad guy with bipolar was walking around yelling   if I see these fucking red and white rags

Monday, 14 September

you're all fucked here the thing is the people arrived with their backpacks so a bunch of backpacks was dumped in the corridor   and the guards were shaking all those backpacks taking out incriminating symbols from them and he was like I'm going to trample on this if I see it here again if anyone has anything left. we were sitting and trying to listen we whispered names and surnames to the others in the cell to know if there'd been someone we knew among those detained and yes sometimes we heard familiar names…

Monday, 14 September

I hardly slept at night. They brought a lot of people and settled them loudly and rudely. They swore a lot and banged the damn doors.

We were told that both boys and girls were brought, and it feels overwhelming for us. It's like a game of battleship. For the entire month, we were like water, running through fingers, hiding in the sand, turning into a river, and they missed, and missed, and missed. But then they hit, hit and sunk… When I'm out of here, will I get into a new round of the game? I don't want to get here again.

> I was scared because sometimes no care packages and no notes or letters came in although I later found out that my friends did write me letters but they never arrived. there was no connection so I felt concerned that maybe something was wrong with them maybe they'd been detained too and it was even a little scary to be released like I'll go out and what will happen what if they detain me again what if they come up with something else…

on sunday a friend of mine was arrested when we were there he was taken to žodzina right away   and he said that on monday he heard girls singing it turned out that   his female friend was in the cell next to his…

206

already after I was released I came to akrescina to get a document   and I stood in a queue   together with a couple of guys   they told me they'd spent ten days in solitary confinement. they were taken when the march was over they were just caught as they were leaving for some reason they were put in solitary confinement where there were no mattresses no bunks no plank beds and their care packages they told me   were placed close to the cell's door   about ten centimetres away   on purpose so they sat there without books without anything in the cold   they wore t-shirts and had no other clothes nothing for ten days...

> In my morning dream I tripped and fell into an anthill... I feel like crying and whimpering but I have to hold on. We are all in the same boat here, and each has enough resources only for herself, but not for comforting her cellmates.

I was always in a good mood all those days because I knew that as soon as I let it get worse for even a minute it would never be good again   and I could see that   it would make my remaining days there   very hard to live through...

I just kind of put myself together and that's it...

Monday, 14 September

it was very difficult for me because I've been living alone for many years   and for me it was strange that I couldn't leave and had to be around other people all the time. you see in prison if you don't pack it all up inside you if you don't bury it all deep down you're just   what are you going to do can you go out or what or will you sit there and bark at the others? this just wouldn't work…

I could call the atmosphere in our cell some kind of fun   from the beginning. we were chatting   from morning till night for the first few days. but for that atmosphere I would have definitely just buried myself in the sadness and gloom and things would have flown   out of me although sometimes it happened   some memories   would come out   anxious thoughts you know   what worse things could still happen and   that would drive me into a stupor   and it was somehow difficult to get myself   under control…

I haven't written to you all weekend because I had a lot of important things to do:))) Now I can tell you that everything worked out! Saturday was great in the company of wonderful ladies, and Sunday was even better! You'll see everything yourself soon.

208

Monday, 14 September

I saw a very adult woman in the mirror, can you really age, shrink so suddenly? Can it be the clothes I'm wearing here? My body is wrinkled like this mattress and pillow. I enjoy letting my pen run on paper. The letters are resolute, the lines are confident and straight.

I started taking notes and I also wrote a letter to ▮▮▮▮ that I wasn't going to send him and we hadn't said I love you to each other before and I didn't write I love you in the letter but it was clear from the text and I thought that I wouldn't show it to him but I'd save and maybe show it to him someday and I showed it to him later after we were both released the following day he said I love you to me and I didn't answer him but the day after I showed him that letter. it turned out that I was writing him letters and he was writing me letters too we then exchanged them it was also very touching. when you write to a person you think that he will read it and you sort of systematise what happened during the day and you have to somehow process your feelings a little not completely but at least something and it's also useful...

I cleaned the sink with wet wipes, delaying the psychosis a little longer, which is getting closer the more I look at the dirt and the hair stuck to the soles of my pink sneakers on top of the drops of urine.

there were a lot of cockroaches in our cell I guess because the cell was warm so they all came to us...

Monday, 14 September

Three days in, our youngest finally got to smoke.

the girls smoked I smoked a little too because you know it's some kind of I don't know something else something different that you can do in prison to somehow distract yourself some kind of pastime a ritual maybe I don't know what to call it but it just somehow brightened up the everyday greyness. in žodzina you could keep cigarettes in the cell and we had them from the care packages but you couldn't keep matches and sometimes the guards well if we asked nicely could I have a light? they would give you a light like they would stick it in the food slot we would light the cigarette and move long very close the wall to the toilet to the ventilation so that no one would see us on camera. once they made a deal with us like you will now tidy up the cell move away all your socks and underwear take your things off the bars take them off the shelves in the cupboards from the sink too so that everything looked nice and decent then I'll give you a light…

For the rest of the day we're reading
The Bonobo and the Atheist: In Search of
Humanism among the Primates.

I was sorting through the books like what can I send you so they'd allow it and all my books are a little bit either political or the kind that wouldn't be allowed so I wanted to send you something like that with an interesting title…

Morality predates religion. We are social animals and value social connections. Without this foundation, religion could endlessly teach us about good and reject evil — and no one would understand it. We are receptive only because we have developed an understanding of the value of relationships, the advantages of cooperation, and the necessity of trust and honesty...

Monday, 14 September

it was a kind of litmus test because we'd been flatmates only for two months   well we just lived in the same flat and that's it and then at some point you realised that you really worry about the person   and it's a shared experience   and it doesn't matter how long you lived together how close the person is to you   you realise that they need help   and you   start collecting these things   as if for a very close friend   figuring out where to go how to make these things reach them   and there's this sudden leap...

first of all   I made friends with women. I'd never really   got on well with women   even in terms of feminism   I was like I love strong men masculinity   assertiveness   and all that   and it doesn't really fit into the concept of feminism. well for sure I'm for equal rights for women and men and all that but at the same time I myself am   attracted to a more masculine   type. I've always had such relationships with women   not that I   trust them   it's difficult for me   to open up   even physically   it can be difficult   to touch a woman I mean   I   feel unsafe. for example when I'm with my mother and she   tries to hug me   it's always a huge stress for me and I want it to end as soon as possible. but   that whole revolution made me look at women in a completely different way because   in fact we can say that women made it   we were very strong very brave and   I think that many women in this revolution learned a lot about themselves   for example I didn't know that I was so brave   and I didn't know that I could   endure what happened to me   I didn't know that I was capable of defending a man   I didn't know that I was capable of rushing after   my loved one who was being taken away I didn't know that I can do that. but it turned out that I can   and women are so cool and can do it too   and   well it was a happy discovery. you can understand it rationally but   in this revolution I felt it   I finally felt women's solidarity. and   it was   important...

Monday, 14 September

after that I   started treating my colleagues   a little differently   because   it turned out that   they cared about me   and I thought that being detained   was my own problem. I started to treat   my mother and sister more reverently   because there were three of us left three women. my dad was   an ardent opponent   of the regime   and when I was detained I thought   he'd be proud of me. I still wish   all this   wasn't in vain. at some point I was like dad please   help us from heaven because you're on our side too...

there in prison I realised how valuable my family is to me   because   I knew that they are the only people who can help me in this situation   who really care about me   and are definitely doing something although I didn't receive any special news from them you know there was only one care package but still somehow I knew it   I somehow felt it   I also worried about them that they were probably terribly concerned. and afterwards my attitude to them   changed because before that   my relationship with my parents   wasn't so smooth you know I was unhappy   with how they brought me up that they didn't give me enough you know meaningless things   but   after prison I just globally realised how dear my family is to me   that these people are   just   the only real value   these people who have always been with you always supported you   I just didn't fully realise it but in such conditions when   well like you have nothing you are desolate   such situations they set priorities   they showed you who really values you and who doesn't   and I   received support from some friends too sometimes from those I didn't expect it   who noticed that I disappeared   and worried and they were looking for me on the lists   it was very touching very nice and   just yeah   yeah...

Monday, 14 September

I was blessed with cellmates   for example   there was a girl   who wasn't connected   with the national movement before   I wouldn't say that she   had the same views as me for example   like the importance of the belarusian language all that   she worked at a regular job etc. but she developed interesting thoughts you could see that something was being born in her   like thoughts about   the belarusian spirit   how it's suppressed in children from school age   how there's no space to develop it how freedom is suppressed   but in fact belarusians are very strong…

I hope you're in good
company there. It matters.

my cellmates happened to be simply amazing… one sang well and   he spoke german there was a doctor who also spoke german   another one who is an entrepreneur now but before that   back in the nineties he was involved in helping with the adoption of belarusian children in italy so he spoke italian…

Monday, 14 September

100% of my cellmates had higher education...

they decided to mix our cell   and scattered us around in another cell everyone was a political too   one of them from the minsk tractor works strike committee detained at the march   he was indignant that he had to go back to work and complained about how the workers there were impossible to stir up   they were like slaves. he said that some people who work there are open prisoners   who are simply hopeless   they can't do anything at all because if they do   they'll immediately get real imprisonment...

one girl was   from the cascade estate   and when the police were taking down the flags   she blocked their way to the yard with her car   and she was arrested for fifteen days   but actually she did it accidentally because she couldn't figure out which way to drive and blocked the yard. well while in jail she certainly thought a lot   including   about purely human behaviour what's the right thing   to ignore what is happening or not about courage as well and the meaning of prison in her life   prison is a good space for this   of course...

Monday, 14 September

Hanna, I hope you are well. I saw you in a demonstration in the catalan tv news a few days ago. I like that you are experiencing this historic moment, proclaiming for freedom, for a better democracy, a better world. Dangerous but beautiful at the same time. Sending you a big hug. Take care. I really hope you are well. I've just heard in the news that +400 people have been detained today.

Take care ♥

Tuesday
15 September

Nights are the hardest time, on a pillow like a sack of potatoes, on a bunk which is hard and cold, to the sound of metal clanking, to swearing and loud laughter.

Tuesday, 15 September

time dragged on incredibly slowly of course especially at night because at night all normal people slept but my brain started working well I read until about two in the morning there's a light bulb I'd crawl under it and read because if I hadn't been reading I'd have driven myself crazy with all my thoughts and count-downs. I read as much as I could until my eyes got tired then I tried to fall asleep as quickly as possible. there was an older woman on the bunk above mine when she just came she was more or less fine she talked to us then closer to her release date she slept poorly she fidgeted a lot the bunk creaked endlessly and she also started talking to herself plus she had bad eyesight she couldn't read couldn't distract herself by reading and I waited for her release almost more than for my own so it would get a little easier in a moral sense...

I think about you every day. Every little thing now makes me think: how is hanna? Not knowing must be the most painful thing. Even when I stay at home and don't see the world with my own eyes, I start to fade away. And behind bars, it must be really hard. I thought about what could cause me the greatest discomfort. For some reason, the first thing that came to mind was bedbugs in the mattress. They say that a hoodie helps. But as far as I remember, you didn't have one(((

217

We amuse ourselves by coming up with revenge scenarios.

If we could torture with the power of thought, these freaks would be writhing in terrible agony.

How to find out their names, how not let them go unpunished?

How to not be destroyed by this hatred?...

I remember we were laughing there like we were insane   we wrote reports in the style of the news on state tv how they will write news reports in belarus soon   so-called maryia kalesnikava   went on a so-called walk with a so-called support group with a so-called press secretary and they staged a so-called protest   in support of so-called viktar babaryka. so-called opposition so-called women in so-called   white dresses   with so-called flowers in their hands   went out to so-called kamaroŭka...

In the mornings, sadness overwhelms you when you realise that you are still here and you are staying here, that they'll bring you salty oatmeal and awfully sweet tea soon...
And you chase away the question whether they washed the dishes in which they'll bring you all this. I'm a poet, a poet, I need to look for poetry in everything, it'll help, it has always helped. I'm being mesmerised by the tea leaves at the bottom of the aluminium mug, imagining that the tea is a night sea, and the tea leaves in it are fish...

Tuesday, 15 September

it was depressing that there was no feedback from outside with what was happening with my parents and friends...

Sending you rays of our support and love. I'm sure you can feel it!!!!!

Sometimes one of the guards opens a narrow slot in the door and peers into the cell, silently. Like a maniac. That sound is from my childhood, when they took a blood sample: the nurse would prick my finger with a pin, suck the blood through a narrow glass tube, drip it onto a glass plate and smear it — the sound of that tube hitting the glass...

I don't think I was particularly afraid of them only of one guy who came to check us in a balaklava what was that for at all? he was aggressive what did you do why did you draw a heart on the door! because we drew a heart with soap on that slot where they look in and he noticed because you know it shimmers in the sun and then when we washed it off it didn't wash off well there was a mark left. he was like what you drew a heart do you have nothing to do I'll send you to my grandmothers' dachas and you'll have to weed their vegetable garden...

Tuesday, 15 September

paper like for drawing   we made playing cards from it   and on tuesday we were in a kinda good mood   there was some kind of tasty lunch normal like   big portions   and we wrote a   thank you note   thank you for the tasty lunch well we had a rule if they did something well   then we   had to respond well to it if they did something bad we responded accordingly. on tuesday we wrote a complaint because   they   still didn't take us out for a walk   and on wednesday   they came to scold us for the complaint   the boss came   this misha balaklava   so he came scolding us and we are trying to give him a thank you note for the fact that they fed us deliciously   and so we are like we have a thank you note he goes like put away your shitty paper he went hysterical   and threw things around our cell like why would I take you out for a walk   you call this tidy in your house do you have the same?! and he took a few playing cards   because we were just playing   he took a few of those pieces of paper   and it's not just ordinary but stone paper   and it's a little rubberised   so he fiddled with it in his hands   and tried to tear it up   it didn't work   so he crumpled it up got mad threw it on the floor and that's it. and when they were letting us out   he was also walking around there but before that he'd be coming to us in a balaklava   and when they were letting us out he was wearing a mask   and we still recognised that was him…

we were met by   you must have seen him too   misha the riot policeman   they have this officer who never seems to take his balaklava off   he's all in black   tall   stooped   with a really pathetic voice   and he started yelling he called out our names and yelled   the words   he didn't speak them he yelled   and   they led us down those corridors and he kept yelling at us to move faster   and of course we had our bags   with our stuff well   it was   awkward to drag   and that must have kept making him angry…

Tuesday, 15 September

I just tried not to talk to them not to joke nothing. I didn't want to talk to communicate with them or to suck up to them so they would give me a match or something no hee-hee-ha-ha but I didn't want to argue with them either I wanted to ignore them as much as possible I avoided any contact with those people...

out of all of them there was one well let's say quite a nice officer we had a doctor in the cell who spoke exclusively in the belarusian language and that guard tried well he tried to speak in belarusian with our cell...

we tried to be extremely polite and not allow them to treat us the way they were used to treating people and perhaps because they hadn't figured out yet what to do because we were what a second batch after you of educated polite calm women and I think they really couldn't figure out how to behave with us and even at some point they started saying to us please good night and that kind of thing. but I know that those who were polite to us beat people a few weeks later and were far from polite...

Tuesday, 15 September

> When I'm out of here, I'll seek psychological help. I just hope I won't fool myself that nothing extraordinary has happened that I couldn't deal with on my own.

when I was released   that experience   I didn't really reflect on it   I thought everything went more or less easily   but about a month afterwards   I even wrote poems about that experience which shows that it did somehow lodge in me   and   was festering inside but when I got out   at that moment   I had the attitude like well okay   if I had to spend another week in jail for the common cause again   that's alright but I definitely don't want to go back there because in essence you are in the system   when you know that these people   you are dependent on them   they can do anything they want with you   physically and mentally   and they'll get away with it   and you don't belong to yourself and of course   well   I don't wish anyone   to go through this   what for   and in september our experience was much less harsh but there's no way back there   and I can't completely separate   the experience   of that time   from   the further experience of the situation we are in   because it has all been accumulating   including inside me. of course I don't regret it   I didn't do anything wrong I'm not guilty   I didn't violate the constitution   and so on   and that's why   in my case   it's not too bad. all this definitely enriches me as a person in the course of my life   what I'll do with it how I'll deal with it if it'll worry and torment me and so on   depends on the further development of events   both internal and external...

> They took us out of the cell for inspection and made us stand along the wall, our hands against the wall, palms outward. A woman was groping our bodies roughly while the men were watching. Did she care? Did she want to show that she had no sympathy for us? Does she feel herself and her body? When was the last time someone was gentle with her?

Tuesday, 15 September

It's a shame that care packages can't be sent every day(We're putting together a package for you for Wednesday.

we were preparing for the worst that you didn't receive the first care package and so thought   okay   she's coming out on thursday but on wednesday we'll still go and send the package   so hanna at least comes out of there   in clean clothes...

we found out that   you'd been   transferred to žodzina and   of course   we immediately started discussing in the chat   if you got to receive the package that we sent because   they accept them there but do they give them to the detained on the same day or they check them once again   repack and marinate them. we thought well   for two days you'll be there like a queen   in case our first package   didn't reach you...

and when we went to shop for you   everyone kept in their minds their own emergency bags and everyone   bought something for their bag which   their friends could send them   someone bought a sleep mask someone some other thing and well that too well for me it was some kind of a cruel insight psychologically...

223

Tuesday, 15 September

I was like an expert who knew how to do everything right what to buy and what not to buy. everyone was ready to meet you but not to prepare a care package well the thing is we were bringing it to you on wednesday and you were to be released on thursday so it didn't make sense to people but we saw it did to us because it's support and you could pass it on to someone else…

we had a chat where we were discussing your care package and who was going to meet you. I took care of the transportation. we went shopping and bought a sleep mask earplugs some food clean new underwear pink. I got you a pair of socks with flamingos…

choosing panties for you was hilarious we thought that well you didn't have spare ones to change and you needed them but none of us knew your size that's the first thing and none of us knew what style you like so here we are standing and choosing I found the pink ones and I say let's have a bit of fun and make hanna laugh let's buy her pink ones ███ is like no it's not serious let's get her black ones they're practical and so we didn't find anything better we took the pink ones and to go with them I was picking up a sleep mask for you…

it was the weirdest shopping in my life and took a long time we bought little but we had a list and we tried not to forget anything at the same time something new would come up let's get this let's get that but we'll go over the allowed weight the girls were also laughing at me when I was choosing toilet paper I said we have to choose nice soft fragrant paper for hanna and coloured one of course so it cheers her up and I really spent a long time choosing and they laughed at me and said ███ you'll have a hard time in prison…

Tuesday, 15 September

we brought it all to my place and had to sort it all because in prison they won't accept it in the original packaging. I sliced the sausage put it into a bag and stuck a label with the expiration date on the bag. ███████ was doing the chocolates she unwrapped each one and threw it into the bag…

the chat was buzzing people were deciding something looking for trousers or panties and lots of people wanted to contribute it was like a competition like I buy biscuits I bought slippers another one bought something else everyone really wanted to participate somehow…

Outside our window, we often hear men's laughter and cannot understand whose it is. A kind of liberated, joyful laughter…

no matter how suppressed one may be and what conditions they put you in no matter how hard it was one will still look for a way out of a difficult situation yes and in this case the situation is absurd when against your opinion well they actually deceived me I cast my vote but at the same time you know that we're doing everything right which means there's someone who trusts and believes us. in the future I'm more than sure we'll have a free country you will be a free writer I will do my printing business and pay taxes honestly and live knowing that tomorrow you and I people with higher education won't end up behind bars…

Tuesday, 15 September

remember how we   left a message for the boys who were brought into our cell after us   we wrote about the window how to open it   and   something else nice   and stuffed it into   the rolled-up mattresses...

We were shuffled, ▒▒▒▒ was moved to another cell, and the three of us into a cell with five others. Now there are eight of us and a window that hasn't been opened for at least three days.

there were five of us   the girls we were at the same police station with   and   after the trial   they put us in the same cell   and some   high-ranking   guard said that we probably wouldn't be transferred   because we were constantly asking what would happen to us next   we didn't know then that they couldn't just keep us in the temporary detention facility   we naively thought that we would spend our ten eleven or eight days of arrest there   and   on the fifteenth all   my girls   were taken out of the cell without a word...

for me the biggest torture was that they didn't take us out for five days   and we sat in that stuffy cell   with eight of us   and it was hard because we didn't know what to do with ourselves for five days you can't see anything at all   we had a gap in the window that was the only place where you could get fresh air   we all took turns going up there and sniffing the fresh air   you could even look at the field a little bit...

Tuesday, 15 September

the cells stank of course so out of ten bars of soap we had I found the most nicely smelling one and I walked around the entire cell and drew on the walls with it on the iron bunks well because it remained and smelled nice. the cell smelled stale almost like in a basement the window was nailed shut so we asked them to open the feeder for us at least at night to open it a little for some air to circulate...

I remember that cell for eight people the light and clouds of smoke the night when the girls smoked was hell. five girls smoked three cigarettes our window wouldn't open and I was lying there realising that the smoke just stayed in the cell. then we asked the guards to open the feeder a little but it didn't help much...

Hey! Today we counted the days till you're home. As if the number went down because of the counting

Wednesday
16 September

Wednesday, 16 September

At least it's warm in the cell, and for the first time in days I don't need to wear socks. There's also hot water and lots of shampoo, creams and books here.

I feel like crying because I'm used to the atmosphere in our little cell for four, and now there are a lot of new people, and I'm getting a little overwhelmed. But I just lie down after breakfast to catch up on sleep and wake up in a better mood.

we must have got up at 6 am   to come to žodzina early and sign you up on the list for a care package...

I was standing at a bus stop   in the morning admiring the sunrise   and a trio of   homeless-looking alcoholics passed by   shouting   long live belarus! and next to me at the bus stop an old woman   with a very   grumpy look   stood   she's looking   at them   well that's right   only people like these go to these protests...

we arrived   with a care package for you   but there are no cars and no people   okay   we went to the front entrance and there's a volunteer who tells everyone that care packages aren't collected over here but   five hundred metres from the prison   the building of the centre for social protection of the population. there are cars   and people there   we arrived around eight in the morning given that they were supposed to start accepting packages   at ten. we signed up on the list   yours was in the second ten names   the first page of the a5 notebook. well we walked around then sat down   and drank tea   sat in the car and at nine in the morning they started accepting packages we were pleased...

Wednesday, 16 September

there was a ginger cat and ▇▇▇ played with it...

we got lost   at first we went to the prison itself   I was so shocked by the look   of that building it   was so daunting heavy energy   around it   I immediately got very quiet I sat in a corner by the window in the back seat of the car and I just didn't want anything because it was a very heavy frightening place   and I thought about you being there...

I was constantly making and changing lists of what to put in your package and   I was pissed off because on one hand it was good that you had slightly better conditions in žodzina but at the same time we couldn't send packages every day   so we had to wait for wednesday and I worried because I didn't know what you needed   maybe we put the wrong things for you   and you're sitting there thinking and why do I need this stuff...

while we were waiting we wrote messages for you on pads   we used gel pens so we had to dry them   a little and at some point we had an open trunk with two bags in it and pads lying in a row   drying as if we had come there to sell something...

the idea to write on pads was actually ██████'s they didn't accept books back then so we bet on male disgust. cool idea let's write but what to write? I didn't have enough imagination because I didn't have the energy then I was out of breath. I was surprised that alena had a message for every pad that she wrote and drew hearts...

I knew that letters weren't allowed and when I was buying pads I thought they wouldn't check pads. the security guard who received this package he sees when you're to be released he says doesn't she come out tomorrow like does she need so many pads we're like she does she does and she can give it to someone else trust us the pads won't be wasted he's like well alright. we were worried that they would open them and see the messages...

we were also trying to figure out how to ensure that you could read the pads we stacked them one next to the other put a pair of panties in between them and wrapped them up so that if you took them out a pad would come out and you would see that something was written there. it's interesting that the men who received the packages apparently had traditional views because as soon as they saw a pack of pads it didn't matter that there were 18 of them and you were getting out the following day they were like oh yeah yeah this is necessary and quickly put it in the bag as if it was fire. so four rolls of toilet paper is a lot but 18 pads for a day is fine...

Wednesday, 16 September

at nine in the morning one person in uniform and the second in civilian clothes came and they started right on the street there was something like a school desk the weather was not bad it wasn't very cold. we brought our two bags and waited they brought lists with the release date and by the time they called you there'd been more than a hundred names in the notebook so we were glad that we arrived early obviously. we put our two bags on the desk and they were ten kilograms or something we started to sort them...

they didn't want to take a sleep mask and they didn't want to take the crackers I was so angry with them I was like here you're taking this and this too...

they said no to the bottle of water right away because their water isn't bad and it's heavy. we had a lot of clothes two pairs of trousers two tops they are like guys she's out tomorrow why does she need so many there are five pairs of socks the same with toilet paper she's leaving tomorrow why does she need four rolls let's have one they took out some biscuits too sorted the rest and we took half the package back...

Thanks to the collective intelligence and effort, we opened this window, which was literally nailed shut. Luckily, I have skinny arms so I was able to put my hand through the bars. Now we have air, and I'm very proud of us!

Wednesday, 16 September

the girls with the thinnest arms reached through the bars with twisted magazines and began to jam a folded magazine   so the window could open   and still hold...

I felt good in the large cell   I guess because   there appeared more activities of all kinds   and the daily life was very well organised   there was a system like how you wash your hair   the toilet was fenced off   we had like a cleaning schedule   a calendar made   by the girls themselves   plus there was an artist   who gave us workshops and we painted   with watercolours   we had pencils   crayons   pens   and paints. we also made dinosaurs   out of   the soft part of bread...

I just wanted to get out clean. to smell fresh because I slept in those jeans in the centre for isolation of offenders   under those stinky blankets   when I was brought to žodzina I received a care package with some clothes   like sweatpants   and shorts   so I was wearing them all the time   but the jeans were the thing in which I knew that I would be released   I wanted to erase   all those prison memories from them so I washed them   to   you know   get out completely fresh without   any signs   that I'd been there   suffering. and all the girls were like why   they won't dry in time   but they dried   because I washed them several days in advance...

233

Vulnerability,

I carried this feeling with me at every protest, and now it's here with me too.

"Choose any one of these for yourself,"

the guards joke, settling in the newly detained girls.

this happened in akrescina   they allowed themselves to make such stupid jokes something   like   why are you telling us that we are raping you but we aren't raping you now are we   or something like that   or even back at the police station   when we were detained   one of them said   don't worry   I'm just looking for a future wife for myself…

I'm trying to read, but it's really hard to focus because I'm feeling worried, because it's a day before release and I can't think about anything else, plus the others are talking all the time.

the people in the cell for the most part were adults understanding that yes like it's hard for everyone   so there was nothing like aggressive or anything   but that girl of course I remember   that girl. well she's just very young well what can I say like yeah we were all mature girls   but then she came like really   simply put she had a lot of energy   and she was like like a typical child   if you tell her something normal adequate people would just shut up but she   wouldn't because who the hell is going to tell her anything   no one can tell her anything because she's so grown up and independent   and has even been in prison. of course she was a bit annoying yeah...

Care package!

I didn't expect it at all. My friends found a creative way to send me a message — on pads! I'm taking each out of the package, reading it aloud and crying.

We're so looking forward to seeing you (a flower drawing).
Well at least you've been to Žodzina (a building drawing).
Say hi to everyone (a drawing).
You're sunshine! (A drawing)
Everything will be fine!
We are many!
We haven't forgotten about you, worrying and organising things for you all the time. I hope you'll read this.
Hanna, love, hang in there. Soon you'll be with us and free. We all love you loads and are waiting for you.
I've never written letters on pads :) I hope it'll make you smile.
Waiting for you out here, sending you a big hug (and I personally will KILL YOU!) Love you.

Wednesday, 16 September

I wanted to get some message more than anything but there was none the first care package and the second one some books and I keep looking   but there's no message it concerned me and I wanted to cry precisely because of this well because I don't know at least one word or underline letters in a book at least something I was really waiting for it…

my wife   supported me all that time   and sent me another care package   in which   on each page she wrote I love you   long live belarus   and drew hearts   and later when   an IT guy came to my place I said here is a book   there is a message in it   that the fight is continuing   pass it on   because when we are in a confined space we don't control the situation   whether people are still on the streets   so when we found out that the negotiations went badly between putin and lukashenka and the fight really continues   I felt relieved in my soul that we may influence something by being in jail   that we will finally get closer to something…

We received a few board games, so we played Svintus until late at night.

At least the day has flown by, still one more left, 'till life…

We can't wait to see you. Tomorrow we will come to pick up our girl. It's the last night Hanna. Then home, freedom, friends. And I hope you'll continue the fight. I don't believe that they managed to break you or make you change your mind.

Wednesday, 16 September

Tomorrow when they let you out, I'll probably be sleeping. I hope your friends will meet you, hug you and sweep you off your feet with love.

Thursday
17 September

In my dream, ▬▬▬ came to Minsk to see me and saved me from arrest... Even in jail I dream about past loves.

Today I woke up from the timpani of thunder. My first thought was — the last night has passed! We are getting our Hanna! Hurray!!! In just a little while. Memorise it all to tell your grandchildren ☺

I've put on the socks sent to me by one of my friends and feel how close they are. It fills me with warmth.

I remember walking through kamaroŭka   and buying you a bunch of white-red-white flowers   and raspberries   it was so lovely...

it was like   an adventure   like a small   trip. I thought you might have been cold there   so we brought lots of blankets etc   we thought that you weren't fed well   so we bought   some raspberries sweets   that kind of thing   and a bouquet of course of flowers   to lift your mood   for you to see something living and beautiful after these ugly walls. so it was like going to the maternity hospital to pick up a baby   I think the feeling was   very similar...

it was my first time driving to žodzina so you know I even felt kind of excited about the journey and myself at the wheel the road was rutted and it felt like a real journey...

It's hard to stay calm here, because as soon as a few of the guards act appropriately, another alpha male chimpanzee appears and poisons the surroundings with his unbridled aggression.

Then the anxiety returns.

you were to be released and I'd just been taken I kind of already knew at that moment that you were there so when I got a care package well towards the end and on the package they usually mark who it's for and the slips of paper with names on them they were cut out from used paper with lists of people serving their arrest so I tear off this slip of paper that was stapled to my package and I realise that on the back it has your last name and I'm like here we go. I think this is a very poetic moment about the fucking place a person has in this fucked up country...

Thursday, 17 September

The three of us are getting out today, just as when we were waiting in the cell after the trial, with the same anxious feeling of the unknown, but now also with a trembling quiet joy. You are wary of it because you don't know what to expect from this system, which can suddenly change its mind and keep you here. We are discussing how we're going to get home, by minibus or train, hoping there at least will be some volunteers to show us the way.

I just couldn't believe   that someone would meet me right? I said through those who were released that there was no need to meet me   everything was fine   I'll get home on my own   I'm an independent girl   an adult…

Do you hear me! We're coming!!!!

not going to meet you was out of the question I immediately decided that I was going   even if suddenly your friends couldn't pick me up although ▅▅▅ told me don't worry I'll give you the phone number of a girl you'll go by car with   to pick up hanna. your friends are great they didn't abandon me. you are my sister I adore you and I simply had to come for you…

Thursday, 17 September

we were thinking about going all together I considered going too   then dad says I'll go   they might not give you a day off at work   he says I'll go. I say well go   then that girl called and said there was only one seat   in the car. ▓▓▓▓ says mum I'll go   you won't make it with work anyway. I cooked food for you packed everything saw ▓▓▓▓ off and she went…

there were three or four cars   and   a guy who went to many poetry readings and filmed everything on his tablet was in ours and while we were driving he decided to watch your performance from the bahdanovič museum on the tablet   we're like this is a bit creepy shall we wait for hanna because it's like she's already dead watching her recordings…

I'll be out of here in a few hours. To hasten that hour, we sat down to braid each other's hair. Never before have I experienced it as such a sacred ritual. Women of different ages, different characters and with different experiences are sitting on an iron prison bench, braiding each other's hair… A grooming of a kind…

242

we were braiding each other's hair I I didn't know how I could never learn. ▮▮▮ taught us it was my dream to learn how to braid hair in a fishtail I once watched a youtube tutorial but I never succeeded I don't know they do something they weave strands of hair I try to replicate it on myself but it doesn't work you know and I needed a person who would finally show me how to do it. not from the first attempt but it worked small joys like passing on knowledge from generation to generation in such interesting conditions...

before I was out I washed my hair in the sink I put my beautiful dress on and I am going out like gorgeous what twelve days in jail everything is wonderful...

Thursday, 17 September

In the care package, I received sausage, and I couldn't stop myself from eating it although in normal circumstances I don't eat meat. So weird, eating meat in prison, in a police state where we are meat ourselves...

we bought some sausage for you although we knew that you don't eat it but we thought that if you didn't want it at all there'd be someone to share it with and we thought that whatever maybe the sausage would be fine...

we knew that you are a vegetarian of course and we were hesitant to put sausage but on the other hand if not the sausage then some dried fruit but apart from the nuts it's all sweet so in the end we decided to put the sausage anyway and if you didn't want it then someone definitely would...

I didn't come to meet you because I was working but I came to your party with vegan sausage. I wanted to put it in the care package but then I thought what if they steal it? and in general then you'd associate sausage with the prison and I decided that we should nail it down with a positive impression when you're freed. I went to kamaroŭka to get this sausage and then to work happy with the sausage it lay at my working place all day and the smell spread all over my bag...

Thursday, 17 September

*The closer it is to seven o'clock, when I'm supposed to be released, the more anxious I'm getting.
What if they don't let me go?*

They may come up with a new charge and give me a new sentence.

you were released   on the 17th of september   and on the evening of the 17th I was transferred to žodzina but we probably missed each other by   a few hours. and it's very strange   because I   felt the closest to you at that moment   and it was a very strange feeling because it's not the kind of place where I   wanted to experience any such feelings...

it was   a complex operation because   I had to meet your sister first. ███ thought he was the only one driving   and I said sure there's a whole motorcade coming   but we had   the main responsibility to   bring   your sister...

the time   while we were waiting for you   felt so long...

245

Thursday, 17 September

> I was to be out in the evening but my friends and family came in the morning and sat there all day   by the prison in žodzina...

I found it quite amusing to watch   what was happening around what kind of people were waiting   for those who'd served their terms   and yes   these are all people who I want to live in the same country with   they all have these open beautiful faces   filled with some kind of meaningfulness   unlike those   who   work in this institution...

> we arrived and there were lots of people with flowers   all white-red-white   a lot of women were to be out   so everyone had flowers everyone was so joyful   there were really lots of people   and cars everyone got out of the cars   at some point   everyone was standing because well in a moment all our people are to be out...

███████ was teasing the prison workers again   I was again pissed off by that   ███████ was feeding everyone sweet corn   in short this was quite a theatre   of the absurd. so ███████ got well prepared   he brought boiled sweet corn with him   a whole big thing   and it was still warm with salt   and so he was giving the corn away   he also offered his service to take people to the toilet   or to warm up in his car...

> Tension is rising, we were hoping they'd let us out a little earlier, as happened before, but no. We're worried that they have forgotten about us altogether.

Thursday, 17 September

and the head of this prison of this   custodial institution as he called it did us the honour of   coming out to us   you know   such a brave man a real knight he must be thinking of himself exactly like that   like he is no less than a lancelot. and yet he's wearing this   uniform   a really horribly tailored uniform as if   they were wrapped in some kind of rags and   they all seem so old and pot-bellied   not the golden child for sure so   he deigned to come up to us and say in his well-mannered speech this and that   you are guests here   and this is a custodial institution it's a prison yes   so don't joke here and   don't make noise you must move a hundred meters away   and   wait quietly. and with such a gait the gait I can describe as   the master of žodzina...

this boss came out   I started arguing   with him   I didn't have any fear but rather courage I was like come on what are you going to do to me now   this is ridiculous. I mean I knew that we and they were   kind of   in a balanced position   and it even looked like we were actually winning. they asked us to sit in the cars   I remember that it really really pissed me off I couldn't understand   I still have no explanation except that they didn't want those coming out   to see how many people were meeting them how awesome it was. maybe they followed instructions because   there were a lot of people   and the prison guys must have been waiting till it got dark   because there were a lot of people and when you come out and see all these people it's probably awesome and awesome impressions and photos there might have been journalists too so maybe they were concerned about that. he tells me maybe you are a terrorist here he started to tell me something like that   I laughed out loud because I'm standing I have a cup of raspberry in one hand and flowers in the other I say   what exactly   where am I hiding it? I don't know I don't know. then I got even bolder I say   listen we are standing here because we're waiting for our people   who will come out and well they will be happy to see the people   who are waiting for them   he says but how do you know? I say have you ever been jailed?

Thursday, 17 September

and he's like emmm how is that possible I'm the knight here what do you mean jailed I put the rich and all kinds of terrorists in...

then he went to the volunteers who were making some jokes with him holy crap the head of the prison where people are tortured face unfair trials and are jailed you hear about horrible things happening in this place and they're making jokes with him and we were shocked and when he sent the volunteers to us so they'd tell us that we shouldn't be loud here we were again holy crap we were like is this a stockholm syndrome guys don't you understand who you're talking with who you're making jokes with? and they were like no you don't understand arguing with him will only make it worse for the prisoners and that argument just killed us because what do you mean we'll make it worse how can we make it worse with our laughter why don't people just do their job properly? they have a written charter of what and how they should act how prisoners should be kept how are we with our cheerful laughter interfering with the work of this grand institution? it was completely incomprehensible and then he came up to us again I don't know why he did it perhaps he was curious what kind of people there are he's never seen such people. and then it all lasted for a very long time and apparently our behaviour affected whether they released you later or I don't know...

to be honest for me this is an open question about what stand the volunteers who are on duty by akrescina and žodzina have been taking because on the one hand I understand what establishing contact takes establishing dialogue even such a problematic dialogue and I understand that there can be certain moments when it's really better to avoid confrontation and then achieve even tiny progress for your goal but on the other hand sometimes it seems like this is turning into and not only among the volunteers even among us that sometimes it's some kind of worship that even this resistance is sometimes like well with a certain kind of I can't even find the words these guys in uniform treated us as if they were little gods and even when you are fighting this resistance is not with equals but with someone who possesses some other qualities than you...

I'm trying to shove the anxiety deeper, but ▇▇▇, damn it, is contemplating aloud, non-stop, whether her mother will meet her or not, that it would be better if she didn't meet her and that maybe she doesn't know at all what's wrong with her daughter; how we'll get there, maybe this, or that, and what if... I can't stand it. I'm losing it. How much longer is she gonna be talking about it, it's not easy for any of us, and no one here can babysit her... The girls fall silent, and I hear ▇▇▇'s voice, "Wow, this is the first fight in our cell..." I want to sink through the floor.

I was surprised she started talking about her mum although before that she was slagging off that her mum wouldn't even come for her and didn't give a damn at all but then when we moved to another cell and the girls were talking about mothers she also picked it up of course it annoyed me I really wanted to say shut up just shut up...

I'll go by train or maršrutka, and at the weekend I'll gather friends at mine...

we prepared a home party for you some of the people went to meet you outside prison and the others went to your flat and prepared a big spread...

I remember that I had classes and I was waiting for the moment when they were just about to let you out I left the classes and thought to myself so today I need to meet hanna everyone was like she loves cider I was like what's cider I'd never drunk cider. I went to the store and bought cucumbers tomatoes everything vegan then cider and I was walking feeling so happy because I'd bring cider and you were coming out so I entered the flat and the scariest part is when you need to communicate with someone who you see for the first time. at the same time we were chatting with those who went to meet you in žodzina they're like damn we are frozen damn ▮▮▮▮ had already messed with the head of the prison. then we started talking how long have you known hanna someone for five years someone for seven years I was like well we kind of met just in august they were like yes hanna told us about you I was well at least something. then we started decorating the table we put melons and watermelons like a white-red-white flag and we hung the flag so it was visible...

We've packed our things.

We ate our dinner.

We were waiting to be let out right after it.

about six o'clock   they took us down those horrifying corridors   then they put us face to the wall   and started calling us   one by one for inspection   but   they didn't make us undress completely   I was in my underwear and a t-shirt   and   that woman just felt my clothes   well I was ready to do   squats   without clothes I imagined how humiliating it would be   and tried to prepare myself for it   but it didn't happen and   the whole thing wasn't as traumatic as I   thought   it would be   well   and the rest of the time we just stood   facing the wall   tried talking but the guy in a balaklava kept yelling at us not to   that's how the first hour went by   then they took me   to a cell and   I saw my girls and it was   a relief...

The door is opening, we're on our starting marks — but they're bringing in a new girl.

she was taken on freedom square they arrived first and got pulled in. so she told us a little bit about how things were...

I'm looking out the window and it's getting darker and darker and where to go in this žhodzina with these bags you'll stand there and cry because the minibuses probably won't be running so late nor the trains and you'll spend the night so it's better to be out tomorrow when it's light you're all packed up and ready the door opens and they bring food well cool we'll eat and go then the door opens again a new person we're like and us? shut your mouth and sit. they brought this girl she started telling us something and you kind of listen but not really she was also standing by the window and you kind of see that it's dark out there and you're in this žodzina...

And we're finally getting out!

Thursday, 17 September

the door opens   quick! because they were behind schedule   quite a bit behind schedule the tenth day started for us...

they were letting us all out at the same time   that's why I met people I knew from akrescina   so we were like   old acquaintances who haven't seen each other for a long time. there was a mess and confusion   the guards themselves were walking around   irritated and swearing and we   we were already good   we were happy   smiling...

when they were taking us out of there   that corridor seemed endless it anyway felt long and on the way back it was totally endless...

of course these   moldy catacombs through which   we walked   these concrete fucking dungeons   you just want them to end...

when I was getting out I couldn't believe it either   I couldn't believe it are they letting me out? for real? and then those long corridors   thump-thump-thump-thump-thump and well I just   really couldn't believe it...

and   when they were releasing
us those doors   a lot of doors
and you walk you walk   and you
wait for fresh air   to simply be
led out   of this   building...

We collect our phones from the
window before the exit. It's taking so
long, why is this all taking so long?

The last stage —

a square of asphalt in front of the
building, we're standing in several rows.
"I need your autograph,"
I hear a whisper behind me.

we were all wearing masks   but then   they
called your name. I first saw you back in
cafe hrai   there was a poetry reading   you
were performing   and then I came up to
you and asked for your name   so I could
find you   and then I remember you   in line
to the central election committee   when
we were filing an application   then   I saw
you when we were   crossing the street the
tram tracks in mašerava at the traffic lights
then by the courtroom   and then when
were were being released...

I was walking and crying a guy was following me and
he   asked for   my phone number it's cute of course but
you're walking out of prison crying   and someone's
asking for your number well it's just absurd...

when we went out   my god   the air   found my phone   and away...

I'm not walking anymore, I'm running, to get out and forget about it as soon as possible. Nothing bad happened to me, just nine days. I see my friends, I rush to hug them, I cry. "We were well fed," I say, hugging the flowers, squeezing the cup with raspberries. I automatically take shoelaces from ▓▓▓▓▓ to never use them. My sneakers were standing without laces for a long time.

well so when they let you out I thought my god in this hoodie all this time dirty poor thing and you came out so lovely   with a fryzura I thought not bad for a terrorist do they have some kind of internal beauty salon there or what   like powder everyone a little before releasing. but yes it was so good   those moments of small happiness   they happened rarely but but it was good   well then everyone started hugging you   and kissing   and feeding you raspberries...

and also we didn't know if the care package had reached you or not but I remember putting a hair tie   for you in it and I see that hair tie on your hair   phew   the care package had reached you...

Thursday, 17 September

and when you were getting out a guy called out   long live belarus   and everyone replied long live!

you   came out like   stunned   on adrenaline you were crying and laughing all at the same time and   your eyes were shining I don't know as if you were high on something   on freedom   we took a picture of you   I   quickly posted that you were free   we were happy and   in general we were glad that you came out safe and sound   and didn't catch covid and   that   they didn't beat you...

so we arrived and you were supposed to be out by certain time but of course we arrived a little earlier so we are all standing and standing and for a while no one was out so there were a lot of people waiting and we stood and stood and stood and stood and it wasn't warm that day I arrived with a thermos of tea and a blanket so we drank the tea and we had to go to the toilet but we were waiting waiting I remember thinking damn damn what if hanna's out once I leave well I can hold it but then at a certain point two more people joined me with the same need and we thought now or never we went to the petrol station well and they let you out of course just then well you know like in a sitcom. but when you see the person you've been waiting for it's awfully touching...

well you looked pretty fine   not tired   we must have been surprised but alright   we could see that you had been through a lot   and you wanted to share to tell us about it   you were high on what was happening. we could see that you were on adrenaline   and that you'd been around people   all the time it was like a person returning from a summer camp   well I mean there wasn't a feeling   that you returned from a peaceful holiday   but you were coming out of a rather   intense experience. well it was cool   very touching. our lives were different   not like now now we're saving energy   but then you didn't really think twice you did this   went there   during your working hours not a problem easy…

So many people came to support me!

So many people wrote to me during this time. I feel bad for their concern, because I knew that nothing terrible happened to me, but they didn't.

I felt strange when I went out there was an entire operation in place behind the walls   I didn't know   I didn't know that so many people were participating in absolutely everything   there was a whole crowd   as big as that which came to meet me   and even then it wasn't everyone who participated in the operation. preparing care packages   sitting in court   waiting for me in žodzina   and near akrescina…

Thursday, 17 September

but again when you are in isolation you don't know anything I thought well   when I'm out   I'll have to somehow get home from žodzina   but then you get out and there's a whole crowd greeting you   on the one hand it's of course   indescribable on the other hand you realise   what a pleasant feeling it is. you think they must have forgotten you there   collected your things and carried them out the door but then   you come   and everyone's happy to see you   and of course that's fantastic...

Maybe nothing terrible happened to me because they thought about me, talked to me, waited and supported me while I was tossing and turning on the metal railing of anxiety, while I imagined how I would look, flat-eyed, at people who haven't gone through this and won't, while I was staying human...

it broke me into before and after   and   you kind of understand better the people who are still imprisoned   and   in general   you feel much more sadness   because for you it's no longer some abstract thing   that is happening with others   yes people are in prisons   and they are being abused   and you were in better conditions if you look objectively   and you felt bad there   and   because of this it becomes a thousand times more painful to read about all these arrests. say maryia kalesnikava   you realise perfectly well that she is a strong person   and she will have consequences after being jailed for so many years   and you saw with your own eyes a person who   went insane   in just a few days   and like well how can she be in prison   for two years thinking about it is unbearable...

Thursday, 17 September

well you   you are a true intellectual   you are a writer   a poet   it's all about those subtle matters art   and not every person is given this in this world   to create art   it's the most difficult thing you can imagine   creating other   meanings   universes   I think   it's inaccessible for most people and you   walk out of prison   with this childish   and slightly nervous   walk! what's that   how! if it were the 1930s   I don't know   you would have been   killed   I guess and I don't know maybe our other friends too and myself...

it's so strange that   you came out   and   said that you were sitting there in warmth and calm   and we'd been worried and concerned here and you were worried about us...

We returned home, and so many people are there. I've never had so many guests even on my birthday. The table is laid out, everyone is excited, I'm telling stories. My friends are feeding me because I don't feel like eating at all, I don't quite understand what's happening, but I'm telling and telling things loudly, and we are laughing.

Thursday, 17 September

the whole world seemed different like computer graphics   all the colours   nature well I couldn't believe it   and in general like materialisation you know   you aren't you like in some game…

your stories and shining eyes. we hugged and spent a bit of time together   well you looked tired to me   and I decided that it'd be   quite ethical if everyone slowly started to leave so I started with myself…

Thursday, 17 September

When everyone left, I fulfilled two of my dreams: I took a long, warm shower and went to sleep in my own bed, in silence and darkness. Until morning I read the messages that had been sent to me for nine days through all possible channels

Sweet Hanna, I truly admire you!! I can imagine how you looked with confidence and dignity into the eyes of those dicks who jailed you for 9 days! You are a true heroine!!! I was very worried about you, as were thousands of Belarusians!!! So happy to see your photos out of there!!!

Hanna, my dear, all the experiences that happen to you don't and can't break you! I never cease to be amazed at how strong you are. Love you.

Thursday, 17 September

I won't be broken as long as such people are with me.

I remember I came home and felt admiration for how amazing your friends are and how amazing you are...

I'm proud of your friends. after I saw them all how united they are. well done. you support each other and it's very important in life when you have such people around you...

Glad that you are ok, my thoughts have been with you and the other brave people in Belarus. You will win in the end.

just tell me briefly. how have you coped with these past days? has it been not too scary?